T0312176

'James Sale provides a compelling narrative using the language of motivation to truly help people understand themselves and build better, more transparent, organisations going forward'.

Tony Henderson, Account Director, Operator
Channels at Microsoft Limited

Mapping Motivation for Top Performing Teams

Mapping Motivation for Top Performing Teams is the final volume in a series of books that are all linked to the author's Motivational Map toolkit. Each book builds on a different aspect of personal, team and organisational development.

This book, using the Motivational Map, the Team Motivational Map, as well as the Organisation Motivational Map, is a practical guide to understanding how team dynamics and success are hugely influenced by motivational factors, which are not usually taken into account. The book is a deeper exploration of team mapping which occurs in Chapter 6 of *Mapping Motivation* (2015), Chapter 6 of *Mapping Motivation for Engagement* (with Steve Jones, 2019), and Chapter 6 of *Mapping Motivation for Leadership* (with Jane Thomas, 2020). But whereas these chapters only touched on specific aspects of team dynamics, this book covers the issues more comprehensively; it also attempts to avoid replication of materials, although there are bound to be small overlaps. It covers not only how motivations affect team productivity and how this can be boosted through targeted Reward Strategies, but also how 'mapping' provides profounder insights into the four key characteristics of top performing teams: the clear remit, vital interdependency, strong belief, and real accountability. How Motivational Maps covers these areas, we believe to be original, eye-opening and effective in the management of change. Further, as always with Motivational Maps, its language and metrics raise self-awareness at an individual and team level, and so can help resolve conflicts through its common and non-judgmental language.

Managing teams is the key skill of managers: thus this book is a handbook for managers everywhere who wish to excel at management, for without bringing their teams on board (i.e. motivating their teams), they are not effectively managing.

James Sale is the Creative Director of Motivational Maps Ltd., a training company which he co-founded in 2006.

The Complete Guide to Mapping Motivation

Motivation is the fuel that powers all our endeavours, whether they be individual, team or organisational. Without motivation we are bound to achieve far less than we really could, and without motivation we will fall short of what we are truly capable of. Motivation, before the creation by James Sale of Motivational Maps, has always been a 'flaky', subjective and impressionistic topic, and so-called 'motivational speakers' are perhaps rightly not considered entirely credible. But the Motivational Map has provided both language and metrics by which motivation can now be fully understood, described and utilised effectively. *The Complete Guide to Mapping Motivation* provides a total overview of how motivation informs all the critical activities that we and teams and organisations undertake at work. This includes how motivation is vital to the individual on a personal level if they want to be happy and fulfilled; it includes its applications in the domains of coaching, engagement, leadership, performance appraisal, team building and organisational development and change. So much has been written in the last 30 years about behaviours that often the literature has missed the crucial point: what drives the behaviours? This new model, then, instead of trying to control behaviours, seeks to understand motivators so that everyone can reach their full potential, not via command and control, but through bottom-up collaboration and appropriate reward strategies.

The Complete Guide to Mapping Motivation is a ground-breaking, innovative and new approach to managing motivation in the workplace. As such it is an essential series of books for all leaders, managers and key personnel engaged in improving how individuals, teams and whole organisations can be more effective, productive and engaged – and how they can want all of these things too.

Mapping Motivation for Top Performing Teams
James Sale

For more information about this series, please visit: www.routledge.com/The-Complete-Guide-to-Mapping-Motivation/book-series/MAPMOTIVAT

Mapping Motivation for Top Performing Teams

James Sale

Routledge
Taylor & Francis Group

LONDON AND NEW YORK

First published 2021
by Routledge
2 Park Square, Milton Park, Abingdon, Oxon OX14 4RN

and by Routledge
52 Vanderbilt Avenue, New York, NY 10017

Routledge is an imprint of the Taylor & Francis Group, an informa business

© 2021 James Sale

British Library Cataloguing-in-Publication Data
A catalogue record for this book is available from the British Library

Library of Congress Cataloging-in-Publication Data
Names: Sale, James (Motivational speaker) author.
Title: Mapping motivation for top performing teams /
James Sale.
Description: 1 Edition. | New York: Routledge, 2020. |
Series: The complete guide to mapping motivation |
Includes bibliographical references and index.
Identifiers: LCCN 2020027265 (print) |
LCCN 2020027266 (ebook)
Subjects: LCSH: Teams in the workplace—Management. |
Employee motivation. | Motivation (Psychology) |
Communication in management. | Organizational change.
Classification: LCC HD66.S253 2020 (print) |
LCC HD66 (ebook) | DDC 658.4/022—dc23
LC record available at https://lccn.loc.gov/2020027265
LC ebook record available at https://lccn.loc.gov/2020027266

ISBN: 978-0-8153-6750-5 (hbk)
ISBN: 978-1-351-25724-4 (ebk)

Typeset in Times New Roman
by codeMantra

Dedicated to
   James Watson, the deep expert, the profound team player and friend

Contents

Figures

Series Editor introduction
The Complete Guide to Mapping Motivation

Following the success of *Mapping Motivation*, a definitive text book on the topic of motivation, it was decided that there was a lot more to say about motivation, and which needed to be said! Motivation is the fuel that powers all our endeavours, whether they be individual, team or organisational. Without motivation we are bound to achieve far less than we really could, and without motivation we will fall short of what we are truly capable of.

Motivation, before the creation of Motivational Maps, has always been a 'flaky', subjective and impressionistic topic, and so-called 'motivational speakers' are perhaps rightly not considered entirely credible. But the Motivational Map has provided both language and metrics by which motivation can now be fully understood, described and utilised effectively. *The Complete Guide to Mapping Motivation Series* provides a total overview of how motivation informs all the critical activities that we and teams and organisations undertake at work. This includes how motivation is vital to the individual on a personal level if they want to be happy and fulfilled; it includes its applications in the domains of coaching, engagement, leadership, performance appraisal, team building and organisational development and change.

So much has been written in the last 30 years about behaviours that often the literature has missed the crucial point: what drives the behaviours? This new model, then, instead of trying to control behaviours, seeks to understand motivators so that everyone can reach their full potential, not via command and control, but through bottom-up collaboration and appropriate reward strategies. *The Complete Guide to Mapping Motivation Series* is a ground-breaking, innovative and new approach to managing motivation in the workplace. As such it is an essential series of books for all leaders, managers and key personnel engaged in improving how individuals, teams and whole organisations can be more effective, productive and engaged – and how they can want all of these things too.

James Sale, Series Editor

Preface

Mapping Motivation for Top Performing Teams is the fifth and final volume in the series, *The Complete Guide to Mapping Motivation*. It is, perhaps, somewhat odd that this particular volume has occurred at this relatively late stage, or even occurred at all, given that a whole chapter was devoted to motivation and teams in the first volume, *Mapping Motivation*; and then again the topic was covered in the subsequent books, *Mapping Motivation for Engagement*, and finally *Mapping Motivation for Leadership*. In each book there was substantially more, and original, information presented on motivation and the use of Motivational Maps in order to develop strong teams or address issues with weaker ones. In short, we have already covered the issue of motivation and teams, haven't we?

True, but in reality we cannot cover the issue *enough* if we want to be serious about organisational development, achieving goals, increasing performance and productivity, and more generally making things happen and making a difference. And just to pick up the first point – organisational development – as long ago as 1986 Charles Handy[1] observed that teams were the basic building blocks of organisational development, and were useful for: distribution of work and developing skills, problem-solving, decision-making, collection of ideas and information and information processing, inter and intra group co-ordination and liaison, management and control of work, testing and ratifying decisions, increased commitment and involvement. And that's just the start!

But there is another, profounder reason why we need to consider teams in much more detail. Bertrand Russell,[2] one of the great British philosophers of the twentieth century noted that, 'Man is not a solitary animal, and so long as social life survives, self-realisation cannot be the supreme principle of ethics'. We have become in the last 50 or so years quite obsessed in the West with the notion of personal development; indeed, the model which has come to symbolise it more than any other (despite claims that it has been superseded by newer models) is Abraham Maslow's Hierarchy of Needs.[3] The very apex of this model is 'self-actualisation', which is pretty much the same as Russell's 'self-realisation'.

The rise of coaching itself as a major and mainstream industry testifies to the importance of the individual and their realising their 'full potential'. And pointing this out is not to denigrate it: Motivational Maps was originally designed to help the individual realise their capabilities, as well as helping the coach to help them too! But it soon became obvious that the individual alone could only deliver so much, but not enough; that teams were absolutely crucial – not only for enhanced performance, but also for that cohesion that comes from a sense of belonging, and so of identity. Paul Martin in his magisterial survey of The Sickening Mind[4] commented as long ago as 1997 that 'We shall all be consultants before long'. Given his context of 'there is no longer a job for life': on the one hand this suggests a stepping up of the work force to new levels of expertise and autonomy; but on the other it suggests isolation and alienation as we become increasingly distant from each other. And we see that Martin was not wrong: there has been an explosion of consultancy services throughout the world since he wrote his book, and a vast extension of the domains where it is now 'appropriate' to be a consultant.[5]

Motivational Maps for teams, then, was developed quite quickly after the individual Map was established, for it recognised the importance not just of the individual's motivation but what collectively the motivational profile indicated. One of the central observations from early-on was simply the fact that so many so-called 'personality' conflicts within teams were nothing of the sort: they were motivational conflicts; they were where the energies between people were running in diametrically opposite directions, and there seemed to be no way to reconcile these tensions.

Furthermore, very early on Motivational Maps realised that there was a vital, crucial distinction to be made between what we often call a group and what organisations and businesses usually want, which is a team; and that it was too easy to settle for groups and pretend that they were a team. The mechanism by which this pretence occurred – and still occurs – is the familiar one: nomenclature. Stick a title on something and somehow it has been magicked into existence: the sales team, the finance team, the operations team; and if we extend this logic, even when we don't use the word team (as in, for example, the use of words like group,[6] department, faculty, unit, division and so on), we still imagine that that is what we have – a fully-functioning team whole heartedly devoted to its specialism. But the reality is invariably otherwise.

We want teams; we need teams; and if we wanted a really simple way of expressing this, we could do worse than going to the sadly deceased Bee Gee, Maurice Gibb! Commenting on the creative power and success of the three Gibb brothers who comprised the Bee Gees pop group, he said: 'One of us is OK, two of us are pretty good, but three of us together are magic'. That is what we are looking for: the synergy between people that produces an unstoppable magic – in business, in music, in virtually any aspect of human life. They worked as a real team; and when they stopped working as a team – as is well-documented in their various split-ups starting in the late 1960s – they were nowhere near as successful, either in commercial terms of record sales, or even in quality of the music and its wider appeal.

Perhaps the real beginnings of the need to understand how teams actually work, and how crucial they were, began in the 1980s, although of course there were plenty of studies before then, but often using the term 'group', as in T-groups,[7] or 'group-think', and such like. Belbin was a famous researcher of the 1980s whose work led to the creation of the Belbin Inventory, an important discovery surrounding the importance of realising that there are complementary roles within a group and their bases need to be covered if we are to achieve teamwork. Writing in the foreword to Belbin's book, Anthony Jay[8] notes that 'while not ignoring or neglecting the individual, we should devote far more thought to teams: to the selection, development, and training of teams, to the qualifications, experience, and achievements of teams, and above all to the psychology, motivation, composition, and behaviour of teams'. Notice that word, which slips into the 'above all' category of attention: motivation. Whilst Belbin's book is fabulous and important still, interestingly his own index at the back of the book does not contain the word 'motivation'. It's like, everyone points to 'motivation' as a key factor but then moves on to discuss 'more important' aspects of building a team.

Lest this be thought fanciful, take another great text from the 1980s: the book *Super Teams: A Blueprint for Organisational Success*,[9] and produced by researchers at Ashridge Management College, which was one of leading centres for management at the time. To create a 'super team' (or what we are referring to simply as a real team, as opposed to a group of people) they identified 20 qualities it needed to have, and again we find that motivation is not one of them. Indeed, motivation has only one citation in the index, although the word does appear some eight or nine times; but motivation is understood by the authors as something 'that comes from being successful'. This view of motivation – which is still common – is a cart before the horse perspective: motivation, they are arguing, derives from success, whereas we think motivation causes success, or more accurately, is an essential component in the real success that results from true productivity.[10]

Of course, lessons have been learnt, haven't they? We are not in the 1980s now; that was over 30 years ago and this is the current situation. But if we could genuinely compound all the organisations, corporations, companies, institutions, teams and individuals who have said 'lessons will or must be learned', and imagine that they actually had been, and that the expression was not some meaningless cliché, then we simply would be in a world where there were no problems, for – obviously – the lessons would have been learnt. Alas, we are not in such a world. For whether it be 30 years ago, or 2000, the problem persists, as Petronius Arbiter[11] noted: 'We trained hard ... But it seemed that every time we were beginning to form up in teams we would be reorganised. I was to learn later in life that we tend to meet any new situation by reorganising, and a wonderful method it can be for creating the illusion of progress while producing confusion, inefficiency and demoralisation'. In other words, there seems to be a general principle of entropy at work and that actually to achieve 'teams', that is high performing teams, is a constant and persistent issue; and it does not go away because we have formed one at one moment of time.

Indeed, if we have taken on board what I am saying here we realise why all the solutions to creating high performing teams over the last 30 years have been – shall we say? – not wholly effective: because they do not address the motivation issue. Motivation is an energy, it changes over time; it's like people – it's something we have to constantly examine, like our health. It's not something we should ever take for granted. But that is exactly what happens.

Belbin, as I have said, is great – it makes sense to look at 'roles' within a team and this can help. But roles are a static concept: have we got the appropriate person in the appropriate role and have we got all our role-bases covered? Yes. But where's the energy? Where's the movement that underpins activity, which underpins achievement and success? And what happens as roles subtly, or not so subtly, shift?

I could cite lots of other 'systems' for developing teams and they all have the same short-fall. To take, perhaps, just one, and the most wildly successful 'team' solution of the last 15 years, then consider Patrick Lencioni's best-selling *The Five Dysfunctions of Teams*.[12] This is another 'solution' and a really interesting book. Its first paragraph could be an epigraph for this study: 'Not finance. Not strategy. Not technology. It is teamwork that remains the ultimate competitive advantage, both because it is so powerful and so rare'. Wow – isn't that wonderful?

But what is the model? Certainly one I approve of in general terms: it is reversing the five deadliest problems that beset teams. Namely, absence of trust, fear of conflict, lack of commitment, avoidance of accountability, and inattention to results. This, like Belbin's roles, is another checklist of nouns – things – that we have to pay attention to. What about trust, conflict, commitment, accountability and results – where are we with these? Where do we want to be? How will we get there? And so the process goes on. But where is the motivation – not the static noun, the thing – but the motivating, the to-motivate, the verb which is about change and flow between people?

This is what Motivational Maps offers. I am not going to pretend this is easy, because it is exactly not that: it is not a magic pill, or a 'do-this-job-done' kind of process, which the 'nouns' tend to be. This is a deep change process. As Roger Harrison[13] observed, 'The deeper we intervene, the more we impact core values and self-concepts'. Motivational Maps require we do just that because we are working with the change in people; this is frightening in some senses, and some employees, never mind employers, will run terrified by the prospect. But I believe, as does the Motivational Mapping community, that 'Work is about a search for daily meaning as well as daily bread, for recognition as well as cash, for astonishment rather than torpor, in short, for a sort of life rather than a Monday to Friday sort of dying'.[14,]

We are looking for a different way of working, one that reverses the tendencies of the last few decades, and some of its unintended by-products. For example, recently Gallup found that 87% of employees were disengaged! That is a startling figure, prompting Derek Thompson[15] to observe that 'one solution would be to make work less awful'! Yes, that would be good! In the UK[16] we find that 'Since the 2008 financial crisis, the UK's productivity has barely budged ... perhaps the productivity puzzle is explained by lack of motivation. People are working longer and longer hours, in jobs that are increasingly insecure, for organisations focused solely on the bottom line. Is it any surprise that many workers feel demotivated?' No, it is not surprising; and notice the word motivation creeping in here too.

How are we going to address motivation; and especially how at the team level? For if we could do that we would have seriously high performing teams. Steven Landsburg[17] observed that 'Most economies can be summarised in four words: 'People respond to incentives'. The rest is commentary'. Motivation, then, is the energy and so finding out the motivators of the team is the task, and having done that the need is to supply the relevant incentives based on the motivators, at an individual and a team level.

What I am advocating is what Dr Alan Watkins[18] suggested: 'Coherent Enlightened Leaders will therefore not only recognise that the troops are in an emotionally different place from them, which is itself a skill, but will have sufficient emotional flexibility to offer different emotional input depending on where the team is on the roller-coaster of change'. The thing is, these are very advanced skills to accomplish without a specific tool such as the Motivational Map. Motivation is emotional, is fed by emotions, and emotions change over time. We create, then, a window with this product to see into the individual and the team at a profound level. At the same time as we see, we can also incentivise appropriately, which is to maximise motivation, and by repeated and regular use we can monitor motivation.

Finally, then, it needs saying that this is not your traditional, conventional 'top performing teams' type of book. By which I mean, a book full of glamour and glitz, involving the famous high-tech organisations that everyone adores, and ooh-aahs about in the popular business pages: we had a problem, we did this, problem sorted, and look how wonderful we are now. You too can be like us! No, the focus of this book is on change and ambiguity, and one thing this focus does highlight is how we can go forward, but also how easy it is to go backwards. It is also less about the well-financed corporates and more about how Small and Medium sized businesses cope with change. The principles, however, are applicable to any organisation. I have ransacked my extensive collection of case studies (all anonymised), sometimes going back a long way, in order to show some fascinating insights into motivation and change that beset and perplex the unwary. This book really is for those who want depth of understanding, not just an easy fix.

Therefore, some of these examples and case studies are hard, but there are plenty of activities to encourage thinking, as well as doing, and the abundant Figures provided by Linda E Sale will I hope provide much clarity into what I am talking about. With these thoughts in mind, now read on!

Notes

1 Charles Handy, *Understanding Organisations* (Penguin, 1993).
2 Bertrand Russell, *History of Western Philosophy* (Routledge, 1946).
3 In *A Theory of Human Motivation*, Maslow says, tellingly, 'I should then say simply that a healthy man is primarily motivated by his need to develop and actualise his fullest potentialities and capacities' (Wilder Publications, Inc., 2013). Of course, 'belongingness and love needs' occur midway up the hierarchy, but stopping 'there' suggests an incompletion of one's humanity.
4 Paul Martin, *The Sickening Mind* (HarperCollins, 1997).
5 And to be clear here: by 'consultant' we mean any individual who works for themselves and trades on their expertise – coaches, counsellors, therapists, trainers, mentors, etc.
6 The word 'group' is perhaps the trickiest to by-pass. For example, in his excellent book, *Psychology in Business* (Lawrence Erlbaum Associates, 1987), Eugene McKenna does not refer to teams, but has a whole and fascinating chapter on 'Groups'. This reflects the psychological background from which he is coming, and its large research base on the topic of 'groups'; however, we insist that the word teams is far superior when thinking about organisational development and success. The most obvious reason being the connotations of a word and the expectations that specific words generate. The British Athletics Team sounds far more focused than the British Athletics Group! Teams, essentially, want to win, whether that be against other teams or against some standard or challenge; groups, on the other hand, simply have to be. Compare: there is a team in the park, with there is a group in the park.
7 See, for example, *Group Training Techniques*, edited M.L. Berger (Gower Press, 1972).
8 R. Meredith Belbin, *Management Teams: Why They Succeed or Fail* (William Heinemann Ltd., 1981/1985).
9 Colin Hastings, Peter Bixby, Rani Chaudry-Lawton, of Ashridge Management College, *Super Teams: A Blueprint for Organisational Success* (Gower, 1986; Fontana Paperbacks, 2nd edition, 1988).
10 I make this caveat because we all know that certain individuals and organisations can become successful through luck or chance. As it says in the book of Ecclesiastes, 'I saw something else under the sun: The race is not to the swift, nor the battle to the strong; neither is the bread to the wise, nor the wealth to the intelligent, nor the favour to the skilful; rather, time and chance happen to all', chapter 9. Verse 11. However, while true, those who become successful in this way seem far more likely to lose their winnings more easily, as, for example, the history of 'lucky' lottery winners appears to show: According to

Fortune Magazine: http://for.tn/1T3cgwU. 'Indeed ... that lottery winners frequently become estranged from family and friends, and incur a greater incidence of depression, drug and alcohol abuse, divorce, and suicide than the average American'. The Certified Financial Planner Board of Standards says nearly a third of lottery winners declare bankruptcy meaning they were worse off than before they became rich.

11 There is some dispute as to whether these are his words: according to https://bit.ly/2YezEBn they are falsely attributed to Gaius Petronius Arbiter. The quote is from Charlton Ogburn, Jr. (1911–1998), in *Harper's Magazine*, 'Merrill's Marauders: The truth about an incredible adventure' (Jan 1957). However, the principle holds true and I imagine everyone who has had real world work experience recognises, ruefully, its accuracy.

12 Patrick Lencioni, *The Five Dysfunctions of Teams* (Jossey-Bass, 2002).

13 Roger Harrison, *The Collected Papers of Roger Harrison*= (McGraw-Hill, 1995).

14 Studs Terkel, see https://bit.ly/2Yis0Wu

15 Derek Thompson: 'Gallup found that 87% of employees were disengaged ... one solution would be to make work less awful.' *The Atlantic*, cited in *MoneyWeek*, 08/03/2019.

16 Jeremy Renwick, capx.co, *MoneyWeek*, 08/03/2019.

17 Steven Landsburg, *MoneyWeek*, 08/02/2019.

18 Dr Alan Watkins, *Coherence* (Kogan Page, 2014).

Acknowledgements

We would also like to thank all the licensees of Motivational Maps – over 800 worldwide; and especially our Senior Practitioners: Bevis Moynan, Carole Gaskell, Kate Turner, Jane Thomas, Susannah Brade-Waring and Heath Waring, and Mark Turner who keep the flame full and burning.

Behind the scenes James Watson and Rob Breeds have provided invaluable support and advice and we are very grateful. Also, thanks go to my son, Joseph Sale, a non-executive director, and writer/writing coach, who has strenuously promoted this series of books through his blogs and social media commentary.

Linda E Sale, the artist, and Managing Director of Motivational Maps Ltd., has to be thanked for support and faith in the creation of this work so far reaching it cannot really be described; but what can be described is the fact that all the Figures in this book, and the cover illustration too, are her work. We are truly grateful – and in awe of her abilities.

It is important, too, that we recognise the superb work of our Senior Routledge Editor, Kristina Abbotts, whose faith, confidence and help in this has been exceptional. Also, Alison Jones whose proofing skills amazed me.

Thanks, too, to Professor Duncan Brown for giving permission to replicate his work in our Figure 2.7.

Introduction to *Mapping Motivation for Top Performing Teams*

Our introduction to *Mapping Motivation for Top Performing Teams* begins where our introduction to the leadership volume began: with a disclaimer! Essentially, building great teams and leadership are similar in that they are complex, multifaceted activities requiring a full range of human intelligence, insight, knowledge and skills to accomplish. Therefore, any one book can only cover so much; as our Preface has hopefully made clear, our perspective here is not to detail all that could be said about top performing teams, but to focus – like a laser – on the motivational component of team building that Motivational Maps considers woefully under-investigated, under-explained and so rendered in-actionable. That after all is the key: action. Theories are fine, but endless theorising leads to academic stultification and no progress in the real world at all. Cicero observed[1] that it was 'the function of wisdom ... to discriminate between good and evil', and so to have ideas but no practical solutions, surely, is a form of evil in that people are left floundering around in their own lack of productivity and poor performances.

And I mention lack of productivity here very specifically, because especially in the UK this has been a problem for more than 10 years. It is estimated[2] that productivity grew by 2% in total over the period from 2009 to 2019, whereas before the financial crisis of 2008 it had grown by 2% per year! High productivity is a by-product of top performing teams; and the thing about it to consider is that productivity is simply leveraged performance(s). Each individual is enabled to perform at a high level – to reach their personal best – but wonderfully, over and above their individual performance being itself productive, the collective performances (the team's) has an amazing synergistic effect out of all proportion to the numbers.[3] We will look at this in more detail later.

But also recall Peter Drucker[4] who observed that, 'No institution can survive if it needs geniuses or supermen to manage it'. Actionable ideas will be, by their nature of being actionable, practical, useful, easy to understand and swift. The promise of building top performing teams is that whilst we do need intelligence, insight, knowledge and skills, we do not need to be geniuses or super-people; we need to be honest, diligent learners who seek to help achieve results and also to develop their fellow human beings whom we call our co-workers or colleagues. And we need these honest, diligent learners to be motivated and therefore highly motivating in everything they do. This, then, is a study about creating motivational teams through having motivational managers who fully understand motivation and how it works.

Since we are going through a new revolution in the work place, this issue of approaching top performing teams via motivation[5] has never been more important. More than 150 years ago we underwent the Industrial Revolution, and now we are experiencing the Digital Revolution which is almost certainly going to have as dramatic an effect on the future as the Industrial Revolution did before. A recent report by Deloitte[6] discusses the disruptors to the world of work: increasing automation and AI technologies, workplace relocation and the move away from traditional places of work, and finally the work force itself becoming more heterogeneous, as in less mere employees, but more a combination of, and interaction between, different worker/talent types (e.g. employees, gig workers, contractors, crowds).

All of this leads to some fundamental shifts. Deloitte instances six major shifts that its research indicates need to happen. First, they head up the whole thing as being about organisations which are 'adaptable' in future; and, to do this, organisations will have to switch from being:

Profit-driven	to	purpose-driven
Internally focused	to	customer focused
Hierarchically structured	to	flexible network of teams
Siloed, bureaucratic interactions	to	collaborative, agile governance
One-size-fits-all talent management	to	individualised talent engagement
Resistance to change	to	change & learning are continuous

They also comment that organisations will have to consider 'Employees are your first customers' and that 'high performing teams' will be enabled 'by adopting connected ways of working and an adaptable culture'.

As you can presuppose from my account above, I am extremely impressed by Deloitte's research, but equally I am also disappointed. For in a 40-page document there is one word missing: motivation! Every buzz-word is used, except the one word that would really make a difference – motivation is not mentioned once in Deloitte's report. It's as if they think that by their analytics and data alone, they can re-shape an organisation. Indeed, they talk of 'reshaping culture and behaviour to act with agility & collaboration'. And this is exactly what the psychometrics do: it's a top-down approach which paradoxically claims to empower the work force. It means we are going to coerce 'right' behaviours and it is, therefore, staggeringly misconceived. At the beginning of the report we learn that '92% of organizations are not correctly structured to operate in this new environment [of the future]' and my estimate would be that in another 10 years' time another 92% will not be correctly structured either, because the whole approach is wrong.

In not addressing the bottom-up motivational approach organisations will never solve their people issues,[7] although that may be good news for big consultancies in the same way that regional wars across the world are great news for various defence industries and corporations. Everyone has their job for life – their profits – and there is no change. And that is a real issue; there is an appearance of doing something about the rate of change, about change itself, and there is whole new line of jargon appearing that majors on this theme – the word 'adaptability' for example being just such a one. Carl Frey and Michael Osbourne[8] recently observed that 'Resistance to technological change does not just come from workers fearful of their jobs but from conservative elites who fear disruption to existing hierarchies'. How brilliant, then, to appear to be championing change but never addressing the real motivational issue underpinning it.

Anaïs Nin more generally commented on life[9] that it is 'a process of becoming, a combination of states we have to go through. Where people fail is that they wish to elect a state and remain in it. This is a kind of death'. Top-down management invariably does this: it seeks change whilst simultaneously seeking to preserve things as they are. The poet WH Auden[10] expressed it this way:

We would rather be ruined than changed.
We would rather die in our dread
Than climb the cross of the present
And let our illusions die.

And that – climbing the cross of the present – is what is required. Motivation is about flow states, and so works with change.[11]

If that sounds too abstract, then let's boil it down to the simplest type of proposition, and let's grasp the full import of William Kendall's smart observation[12]: 'Building a vibrant company is about forming a good team... You cannot do it on your own.... It is a question of persuading people who are better than you to form a successful team'. People better than you? Ah, there's the rub. Who can accept that easily in a culture where – as, say, in television programmes like The Apprentice[13] – we have to prove we are the best? So this is a psychological or ego issue, and one very similar to the whole thrust of what we have been saying all along: namely, that bottom-up is necessary and better than top-down in terms of long-term results and productivity. But again, psychologically, managers and leaders[14] seem unable to let go of the need to 'control' their people.

But let's add another layer to this analysis. For when it comes to teams, as well as individuals, we need to consider rewards. This is an easy to understand concept because it is soft-wired (if not hard-wired) into us from childhood onwards. If we perform, then we get prizes: be a good boy or be a good girl, and we get the ice cream or material reward; but even more important are the immaterial rewards we accumulate – acceptance, praise, admiration, support and more besides, including even love.[15] We want – are motivated towards – these rewards. Organisations recognise this and many now have moved well beyond the simple and simplistic idea that paying people money is enough. However, this movement is itself not sufficient, since it tends to be about the WHAT and not the HOW, which is possibly even more important.

So, rewards are, on the one hand, a content – somebody receives 'something', which is a WHAT (for example, a pay bonus, a trip to the Caribbean, time off, and so on) – but also, critically, it is a process: the employee is handled in a specific way, and HOW this is done is crucial. Naturally, and as one would expect, most organisations spend most of their time focusing on arguably the less important of these two elements of rewards: the content. Content – the WHAT – is easy: make a list and dish out the goodies![16] Who wants to spend a lot of time thinking about it? But, of course, it is HOW we reward people that is more fundamental, and this does take some thinking about. And isn't that obvious? The best gift in the world to one's life partner left unwrapped and casually lying around will usually have less impact than a much more moderate gift – but carefully thought through and based on an understanding of the desires of the recipient – carefully and beautifully packaged, and presented at exactly the right psychological moment.

Moreover, a moment's thought about what motivates us in our dealings with other people reveals that we prefer rewards that are:

Genuine – in that we feel we have really earned them and that we are not being fobbed off

Sincere – in that the person awarding the reward believes in our right to it

Well-intentioned – in that the person awarding cares about us, as in sincerely cares

Thoughtful – in that the reward itself is appropriate and commensurate with the performance

Structured – in that the reward is part of an ongoing pattern or design of positive experiences

Temporal – in that this specific reward is only a pledge of further, greater rewards in future

Any team leader, then, needs to ask themselves whether they are genuine, sincere, well-intentioned, thoughtful, structured and temporal in their approach to rewarding and dealing with their team members. And it would appear that these qualities need to be established at the recruitment or interviewing stage of any appointment for someone who is going to be a leader. For of course, there is no use asking anyone at interview: 'Are you sincere' or 'Are you genuine' because the answer will be 'Yes'! But the fact is, past behavior is a good, though not infallible, indicator of whether these things are so. For more on Reward Strategies see Chapter 2, and on recruitment as a core asset for top performing teams and how to go about it motivationally, see Chapter 6.

This book unpacks four simple ideas from a motivational perspective: that top performing teams have or practise four characteristics: the remit's clear, they practise interdependency, they have strong and specific beliefs, and they are accountable. Simples? Yes and no. The topic of The Remit alone takes up three chapters – 3, 4 and 5 – as we unpack three particular dimensions of it. And the remaining three chapters cover the other three areas of Interdependency, Beliefs and Accountability. Motivation at this point might be compared with knitting: there are certain threads and 'weaves' that come back time and again, or crossover from one characteristic to another. Furthermore, the usefulness of this book is in the relentless motivational focus it follows.

We could take the obvious lists like the one we have just listed – Genuine, Sincere, etc. – and ask for people to rate themselves and from that try to spot what is missing, and subsequently devise exercises around it. But where we can, we avoid that, and stick to the motivational issues, tools and techniques. One marked exception to this rule occurs in Chapter 7 where we introduce the classic NASA experiment, which is so relevant to team beliefs. There is always an exception!

Finally, because motivation is emotional, and is inherently about change, the case studies tend to be 'messy'; there are no easy solutions. As soon as one has turned round a poor team, someone leaves, is poached, external circumstances change, disaster strikes (Covid-19 as I write this), and the whole team needs reconfiguring. However, the joy is: if we truly understand how motivation works, as these case studies reveal, then we are prepared for anything, and nothing should surprise us. We have the language and the metrics to measure, monitor and maximise motivation to its greatest effect – enhancing performance, increasing productivity and ultimately enabling more value or more profitability.

With this in mind, then, read on – explore the world of motivation and top performing teams!

Notes

1   https://bit.ly/2MquM5U
2   Philip Aldrick, writing in the *Times*, cited in *MoneyWeek*, 12/4/2019. Various reasons are proposed for this, including measurement errors, poor investment, regional neglect, low interest rates keeping so-called zombie companies alive and 'lousy' management. It is in this last category – 'lousy' management – that we express our interest, for it is precisely 'lousy' management that creates and sustains poor performing teams.

3 As we review this for publication, we are in the middle of the Covid-19 pandemic. The effect of this on teams and on productivity is at this point unknowable. According to John Authers on Bloomberg, pay rises are a key side-effect of pandemics (*MoneyWeek*, 10/4/2020), and according to Gerard Baker, writing in the *Times*, 'Matters of life and death occasion more drastic shifts in policy than economic indicators ever can' (*MoneyWeek*, 27/3/2020). However that may be, Fred Wilson notes that, 'The key to success at this stage comes down to two things: team and strategy. That may sound simple, but it's not' (*MoneyWeek*, 14/10/2016).

4 Peter Drucker, cited in *MoneyWeek*, 24/12/2015.

5 A recent report from Eden Springs found that some 50% of the UK workforce lacked motivation (http://www.talk-business.co.uk/2015/11/05/over-half-of-uk-workers-lack-motivation/). Peter Sullivan-Stark, head of marketing at Eden Kafevend, comments, 'Our survey paints a worrying picture and it is concerning to think the impact low motivation could be having on productivity levels. We have all heard about the impact that sickness absence has on business – according to the Office for National Statistics, 131 million days were lost in the UK in 2013 due to illness. One can only wonder what low energy is costing businesses today'. And it is estimated that the cost of this to the economy in 2012 was £6B.

6 Deloitte, *Future of Work*, January, 2019.

7 As Marylène Gagné commented, 'Motivation is at the heart of organisational behaviour', *Oxford Handbook of Work Engagement, Motivation, and Self-Determination Theory* (OUP, 2014).

8 Carl Frey and Michael Osbourne, stumblingandmumbling.typepad.com, cited *MoneyWeek*, 05/07/2019.

9 Anaïs Nin, *D. H. Lawrence: An Unprofessional Study* (Swallow Press, 1964).

10 W.H. Auden, from his *The Age of Anxiety* (Princeton University Press, 2011).

11 One way of expressing this might look like, finally: 'A CEO or management team with large ideas and fanatical drive to build their moat. Willing and able to think and act unconventionally. A learning machine that adapts to constant change. Focused on acquiring the best talent. Able to create a sustainable corporate culture and incentivise their operations for continual progress. Their time horizon is in five- or ten-year increments, not quarterly, and they invest in their businesses accordingly. They own large portions of their business. Regardless of the industry, they are able to create moats that competitors fear', *Intelligent Fanatics Project: How Great Leaders Build Sustainable Businesses*, Sean Iddings and Ian Cassel (MicroCapClub Publication, 2016).

12 William Kendall, ex-boss of Green & Blacks, quoted in *MoneyWeek*, 24/6/2016.

13 The general purpose of such TV shows in the UK and America seems to be to humiliate contestants, partly through the judges refining their smart-aleck put-downs and one-liners, and partly by setting contestants up so that they ruthlessly compete with each other; and so a lowest common denominator of success emerges victorious, eventually.

14 We strongly encourage readers of this book also to read *Mapping Motivation for Leadership*, James Sale and Jane Thomas – its prequel – for much more on what is required to develop truly motivational leadership (Routledge, 2019).

15 Strictly speaking, of course, real love we understand is 'unconditional' and not something given for doing (that is, performing), but experienced merely through being. We can love our partner, our child, our friend no matter what they do, but just because they are who they are.

16 As always America has perfected this line of WHAT thinking. Bob Nelson's book, *1001 Ways to Reward Employees*, (John Wiley & Sons, 2001) and its updated sequel, *1501 Ways to Reward Employees* (Workman Publishing, 2012). There are many good ideas in these books – the WHAT – but little on the HOW.

Summary of Motivational Maps
What you need to know in a nutshell!

Within each person there are nine motivators – we all have these motivators, and we all have the full nine; the difference is that each individual has the nine in a different order and at a different level of intensity. This gives rise to the possibility of millions of potential combinations in an individual's profile. Over 70,000 Maps have been completed and we still have never seen two individuals with identical Maps; furthermore, because motivation is partially based on our belief systems, then it changes over time. As it is not static or fixed, it is impossible to stereotype anyone according to their motivators since these will change. Usually, most people are directly influenced not by just their top motivator, but by their top three motivators; rarely, this can be their top two or top four, but the scoring shows what really counts or not (which are motivators scoring > 20).

Motivation is energy; it is what fuels us to do 'things' – things we want to do. Without motivation we are unlikely to set out in the direction we want to go (towards our goals) and are even more unlikely to use our knowledge and skills effectively. In short, motivation is the fuel in the tank of the car we call performance. Thus, knowing what motivates us and how to reward – or re-fuel – our motivators is to enable higher levels of energy, greater levels of performance and productivity, and to seriously increase our satisfaction with life.

The nine motivators are not random or discrete but instead form a holistic unity. They are divided into three groups of three; the groups like the motivators themselves have properties as well as motivational qualities. Some motivators are aligned and reinforce each other; other motivators conflict and cause tension, whether that be at an individual (that is, internal), team or organisational level. The tension is not necessarily a bad thing; for example, it may lead to procrastination – to taking longer to make a decision – but equally this could sometimes mean making a better decision. In Motivational Maps, therefore, as an absolute rule, there is no good or bad profile: context determines the meaning of every profile.

So, to expand and summarise the key principles underpinning Motivational Maps, then there are nine principles to enunciate or express:

1. All Map profiles are good. There are no good or bad profiles – the diagnostic is ipsative, which means that you are measuring yourself against yourself, so you cannot be 'wrong'. What you 'think' can be wrong but how you 'feel' cannot be: it is how you feel; and so it is with your motivation, as they are feeling-based.

2. Context is everything in interpreting Maps. There can be no one meaning isolated from the context in which the individual is operating. Profiles may suit or re-inforce a specific context or not; 'or not' may mean that intention (will power), knowledge and skill will have to accomplish that which one is not motivated to do, or it can mean the difference between focus (the motivators aligned and not closely scored) and balance (the motivators less aligned and the scoring narrowing or close) and which is relevant in a given situation.

3. Motivational Maps describe, measure and monitor motivation. They make our invisible emotional drives visible and quantifiable. At last individuals, managers and organisations can get a handle on this key issue and through Reward Strategies do something about it – namely, increase it. Maps are a complete language and metric of motivation.

4. Motivators change over time. This happens because our beliefs change over time and these belief changes affect how we feel and therefore what motivates us. Thus regularly monitoring of motivation is appropriate and effective. From a coaching perspective this is so powerful because it is a focused opportunity to explore, too, what one's beliefs are, and whether they are supportive of what one is trying to achieve.

5. Motivational Maps are not a psychometric instrument. Psychometric type tools inevitably describe a 'fixed' personality, a core which is unchanging. Maps are stable but fluid over time. Maps take an 'energy snapshot', for motivation is energy. Technically, Motivational Maps are a Self-Perception Inventory.

6. Motivational Maps do not and cannot stereotype individuals. This follows from the fact they change over time, so whatever someone's profile today, there is no guarantee it will be the same tomorrow. That said, the Maps are usually stable for about 18–24 months. But nobody should suggest, in a personality sort-of-way (e.g. 'I'm an extrovert'), 'I'm a Searcher' or any other motivator.

7. There are nine motivators but they are grouped into three types. These three groupings represent, amongst other things, the three primary modes of human perception: Feeling, Thinking and Knowing. Each perception has fascinating and differing properties.

8. Motivation is highly correlated with performance. It is possible to be a high performer and yet de-motivated, but the price for this, middle

| Relationship Motivators | Achievement Motivators | Growth Motivators |

The Defender seeks security, predictability, stability

The Director Seeks power, influence, control of people / resources

The Creator Seeks innovation, identification with new, expressing creative potential

The Friend Seeks belonging, friendship, fulfilling relationships

The Builder Seeks money, material satisfactions, above average living

The Spirit Seeks freedom, independence, making own decisions

The Star Seeks recognition, respect, social esteem

The Expert Seeks knowledge, mastery, specialisation

The Searcher Seeks meaning, making a difference, providing worthwhile things

Figure S.1 The nine motivators

or long-term, is stress and health problems. Having a highly motivated workforce is going to reduce illness and absenteeism, as well as presenteeism (the being there in body but not in mind or spirit).

9. Motivation is a feature and people buy benefits. Let's not forget that because motivation is a feature, then it features in many core organisational (and non-organisational) activities: leadership, teams, performance, productivity, sales, appraisal, engagement (70% of engagement is motivation), recruitment, careers and more beside. People, usually therefore buy the effect or benefit of motivation rather than wanting it directly. Think essential oils! Most often applying an essential oil to the skin requires a 'carrier' oil, so with motivation: it's wrapping the mapping.

What, then, are the nine motivators and what do they mean? The motivators are in an ordered sequence which correlates with Maslow's Hierarchy of Needs. At the base are what we call the Relationship Motivators (R) – representing the desire for security (the Defender), belonging (the Friend), and recognition (the Star). They are represented (on-line) by the colour green, and they are Relationship motivators because the primary concern of all three is people orientation.

Then, in sequence, we have the three Achievement (A) motivators. These are in the middle of the hierarchy. First, there is the desire for control (the Director), then the desire for money (the Builder), and finally the desire for expertise (the Expert). They are represented (on-line) by the colour red, and they are Achievement motivators because the primary concern of all three is work orientation.

Finally, we have the three Growth (G) motivators. These are at the top of the hierarchy. These are the desire for innovation (the Creator), then the desire for autonomy (the Spirit), and at the apex – though this does not imply superiority – we have the desire for meaning or purpose (the Searcher). They are represented (on-line) by the colour blue, and they are Growth motivators because the primary concern of all three is self-orientation.

From this brief re-cap of what Motivational Maps is about we hope that – if you haven't yet encountered them directly – your first response will be: 'That's fascinating – so what is my profile? What are my top three motivators?' To find out more about doing a Map, go to www.motivational maps.com.

Chapter 1

What is a team?

In my book, *Mapping Motivation*,[1] we took our first look at what a team is and how that related to Motivational Maps.[2] We will not cover all that information again, but a brief re-cap is in order.

In *Mapping Motivation*, we contrast a team with a group and insist on the following: that groups can be classified in any number of fancy-sounding ways, but most are usually aligned with their function. So a group can be designated a department, a faculty, a unit, a branch, a board, a committee, a section and so on. It doesn't matter whether the sales department is called the sales team or not: it may be called a sales team but be anything but a team. However, for optimum efficiency and effectiveness we need real teams, not groups. If we want, for example, a committee which is just a talking shop, then fine, a group will do; but if that committee has really got to get things done, then a team is in order and also very necessary.

Before coming on to the distinctive features of a team, let's also keep in mind the specific limitations of a team: authorities vary as to the exact number but we think that 12^3 is the maximum number of members that can be in a team,[4] and once that number is exceeded then the group will fragment; the team cohesion is lost. It is important to realise that simply increasing the number of people in a team does not automatically increase its productivity; in fact, the Ringelmann Effect[5] suggests just the opposite.

Activity 1.1

If you have read *Mapping Motivation*, the earlier book, you may remember the answers to this question, but keep in mind that personnel in teams change all the time. We need to be constantly asking our groups/teams, what are the characteristics of a real, high performing team? Ask any team you work with this question, and jot down your own answers to it. Comparing your answers with those in your team can be very revealing.

My earlier book suggested that there were four distinctive characteristics that enabled a group to become a team.

Figure 1.1 Four team characteristics

Teams have a clear remit, by which we mean a mission, a purpose, something definite that must be achieved. Teams practise interdependency, not independency and not co-dependency! By this we signify that each person's gifts, abilities and talents are needed, are necessary, to achieve the remit or the objective. Not too many people, so there is redundancy and bloat; and not too few, so that there is under-capacity to deliver. Teams hold a strong belief. In what exactly? By this we connote a strong belief in working as a team: that it is better to co-operate – more can be achieved – than to rely on individual effort. Finally, teams are accountable. By this we suggest that team players understand that they are accountable in two ways. First, they are accountable to each other, so that they can rely on and trust each other. Second, that they are accountable to the wider organisation for their results; in other words, they practise the avoidance of creating fiefdoms, silos, autonomous units within that organisation. In this way they minimise friction, conflict, inefficiencies and ultimately ineffectiveness.

Thus, the journey from being a Group, which is more or less random, to becoming a Team, which is more or less structured and purposeful, goes something like Figure 1.2.

We need, then, to encourage the shift from the group state and its attendant long- and short-term problems to the team state where high performance is possible. How do we do this and how can Motivational Maps help? An initial question which we did not deal with in *Mapping Motivation*, or the

GROUP		TEAM
No remit Confused remit Job titles	→	REMIT Mission Objectives
Independency Alienation Dependency	→	INTERDEPENDENCY Belonging Co-operation
No beliefs False beliefs Negativity	→	BELIEFS (in the team) Positive expectations Optimism
Invisibility Distinction (personal) Disruption	→	ACCOUNTABILITY Results Coherence

Figure 1.2 From Group to Team

subsequent books, is this: can a Motivational Map help us identify a weak team, or more accurately a group, in the first instance? Put another way: remit, interdependency, belief and accountability do not on the face of it seem subject to motivational states, but are they?

Activity 1.2

Thinking motivationally, how might a motivational profile have a bearing on whether a unit of people is a group or a team? In order to answer this question, you may wish to review the material in The Summary of Motivational Maps after the Introduction. Also, consider Figure 1.3, which is a Motivational Map for a small IT company (we will anonymise and call it Business on Line Ltd, or BoL) employing seven people, and who create webpages mainly for other businesses. What two or three pieces of information in this Map might provide a clue as to whether this is a group or a team?

Now we need to do two things: first, without having any further background information on this particular case, let's see what the numbers and the configuration suggest to us. Second, if we add some more context, is there anything else the Map tells us? Keep in mind the central question: is this a group or is it a team?

As an initial assessment three things indicate that this may not be a top performing team. The most obvious fact is the motivation of the seven people averages only 56%. This puts them in the third quadrant of motivation,[6]

	Spirit	Builder	Defender	Searcher	Expert	Creator	Friend	Director	Star	Personal Audit			
											1	2	3
Louise Smith	19	27	28	26	20	16	19	14	11	76%	8	8	6
Bob	29	26	16	19	21	24	15	16	14	38%	3	5	5
Tom	23	22	17	24	21	19	22	19	13	42%	4	5	4
Malcom	20	23	22	19	20	19	18	22	17	56%	5	6	7
Max	25	22	20	21	30	26	15	13	8	60%	7	7	2
Mandy	34	23	27	20	20	21	16	7	12	56%	7	5	2
Theo Smith	27	26	22	23	15	13	16	24	14	66%	6	7	8
Total	177	169	152	152	147	138	121	115	89	56%			

Figure 1.3 Small IT company: group or team?

the Risk Zone. Motivation is beginning to drain away and some serious actions need to occur to reverse that; therefore, this seems highly unlikely to be a team.

Second, we do know that this is a small IT company that creates websites for other businesses; it is a B-2-B (business-to-business) type of company. Therefore, we also know that it is a professional company trading on its expertise to create value for its clients. In other words, it is not a standard shop selling common-place confectionary or ice cream! But how committed to expertise is this company? Only one person, Max Eaton, has the Expert in their top three profile, and overall Expert is only fifth. The Spirit/Builder combination of the top two motivators instead suggest a sales-driven rather than an expertise-driven company. So, are the motivators really at odds with the ostensible purpose of the company? If so, that would also suggest a group rather than a team.

Finally, we see with the Spirit as the dominant motivator, and five people with it very strongly in their profiles, plus what we call the 'polarity reinforcement'[7] of the Director motivator being so low, there is every chance that this unit has no real leadership. This point needs some careful unpacking.

So consider: we have three threads of evidence pointing to a group not a team. Put another way, a coach or consultant could without having met any of the members of this team form a reasonably accurate impression of what is going on. The motivation is low – 56% – which practically means energy levels are low, whereas energy levels are usually higher in high performing teams. The motivators of the group are almost certainly at odds with the central purpose (remit) of the organisation in terms of its service delivery to clients. In fact, one could go further: it is highly likely that clients are being 'overcharged' for services, since making money (the classic sales combination of Spirit and Builder) is highly motivating. And the polarity reinforcement is fascinating. Essentially, Spirit (highest motivator) and Director (second lowest) are in conflict: one seeks autonomy and the other seeks control. Thus, if an individual or team had both in their top three there would be an inner tension as one was faced with having to go for more autonomy, and so relinquish control, or take on more control (via responsibilities) and so limit further one's autonomy, or freedom to act. But here they are spaced far apart, which in a sense doubles up the power of the dominant motivator, Spirit, for the Director motivator is not present to curtail or weaken it. This we call polarity reinforcement whereby a dominant motivator is made even stronger.

But that said, in the creation of teams Spirit is one of the more 'difficult team motivators'.[8] If we think, then, of seven people, five of whom wish to be 'free' and quite strongly so (consider the scores: 29, 23, 25, 34, 27 out of 40 maximum) and only two wish to direct and control, and no-one does as their top motivator, then it is apparent that in the absence of strong management, the team is not likely to function as a team – individuals will do their 'own thing' according to their own job titles.

Activity 1.3

We have established purely from a consideration of their Motivational Map team profile that this is not a high performing team. How does this analysis relate to the four key characteristics of a team that we identified in Figure 1.1?

We only reviewed three points evident from the Motivational Map shown in Figure 1.3, but they are telling. In particular, the point about how the motivators may conflict with the work that the company undertakes suggests motivators and purpose (The Remit) are not aligned. Surely, a fundamental issue? Second, the dominance of the Spirit motivator in a group this small, alongside the polarity reinforcement of the low Director, points to independence within the group, rather than interdependence, which is necessary for the team to be high-performing. Further, the same dominance of Spirit also indicates potentially a lack of accountability within the group, either to each other or to the company itself.

In other words, three of the four key characteristics are almost certainly not met and we can know this merely from studying the Motivational Map. The one characteristic that this analysis is not being specific about is the third one: belief. Do they collectively believe in the power of teams over groups? The Spirit motivator alone being so dominant would not answer that question, for what if the team were 88% motivated? Then, we might think there were some significant mavericks in the team but with the right leadership that still might be high-performing; however, here we have the weak motivational score of 56% which rather clinches the notion that there is no real belief. Low motivational scores are usually, but not always, correlated with low performance[9] and productivity levels, and there is nothing here to suggest otherwise. In short (and I think quite incredibly), we can see at a glance, and without reference to any other information about BoL, that this is a group and not a team, and certainly not a high-performing team.

If we now return to this company/team Map and begin supplying a little more detail, we can go even further.

Activity 1.4

Figure 1.4 is exactly the same as Figure 1.3, except that abbreviated job titles have been added and we have added the PMA scores. So we see, for example, that Louise Smith[10] is a company director; in other words, a senior manager of the company. Actually, the managing director, Theo Smith, is her husband, so this is a husband-and-wife, mom-and-pop, classic small

	Louise Smith Company Director	Bob Snr Web Developer	Tom Web Developer	Malcom Business Manager	Max Web Developer	Mandy Admin	Theo Smith Managing Director	Total	Rank
Spirit	19	29	23	20	25	34	27	177	1
Builder	27	26	22	23	22	23	26	169	2
Defender	28	16	17	22	20	27	22	152	3
Searcher	26	19	24	19	21	20	23	152	4
Expert	20	21	21	20	30	20	15	147	5
Creator	16	24	19	19	26	21	13	138	6
Friend	19	15	22	18	15	16	16	121	7
Director	14	16	19	22	13	7	24	115	8
Star	11	14	13	17	8	12	14	89	9
Personal Audit %	76%	38%	42%	56%	60%	56%	66%	Team	56%
1	8	3	4	5	7	7	6		
2	8	5	5	6	7	5	7		
3	6	5	4	7	2	2	8		

Figure 1.4 BoL with personnel and job roles

Bob	3
Tom	5
Max	2
Mandy	7
Theo Smith	6
AVERAGE SCORE	*5*

Figure 1.5 Spirit PMA (Personal Motivational Audit) scores for BoL

business. But given this information, what does it add to our understanding of the Motivational profile? What else might one deduce knowing what each individual's role is within the company? Make some notes on your observation studying Figure 1.4.

A number of important points emerge as we move towards suggestions for improving the situation. But we need now to do a more sophisticated reading of the PMA scores in two ways: first, what their overall pattern begins to tell us; and, second, how the motivators relate to the job roles of individuals.

What we are talking about here is how 'satisfied' are the motivators, especially the most important ones, the top three in fact.

If we study the top motivator, the Spirit, we find that five people have it in their top three. Bob has it as his top motivator with a score of 29/40. How satisfied is he with that particular motivator? 3/10. Not very, then! Now if we take each individual who has Spirit motivator and look at their satisfaction rating, we get Figure 1.5.

Activity 1.5

What deductions would you make from looking at these numbers?

At Motivational Maps we consider 6 to be the 'good' or average score, so here we have 5.[11] So what we are seeing is how the majority of people in the team (and this case the company) feel about the motivator that is most important to them: namely, how much freedom and autonomy do they feel they actually get working for BoL? Clearly, not enough. The deduction we would make is that there is not enough freedom and autonomy to satisfy the team. 7 would be the minimum acceptable number and 8 would be preferable by far. How will this be addressed? We will come to this important question shortly.

But first, there is more here: Theo has Spirit and it is his number one motivator, and yet as leader his score is only 6 – average, OK, will do, but hardly getting the kind of motivation that might seriously energise him. And when we consider that he is overall only 66% motivated, then we know that he is in the Boost Zone of motivation, but not well in; there is a danger of falling back in the Risk Zone below 60%. It is true that he and his wife (76%) are the most highly motivated of all the staff. This is something we frequently comment on as being highly necessary: leaders (in this case the owners as well) are more highly motivated than their employees. But whilst this is good in itself, as being less motivated would be truly disastrous and unsustainable as a business, there are reasons in the Map for suspecting just how 'energising' or motivating their higher levels of motivation are for the rest of the staff.

If we look at the nature of why they are more highly motivated, then something quite obvious emerges: five staff have the Builder in their top three. How satisfied are the employees (not including the owners) with the financial remuneration of the company? Well, the answer is staring us in the face: they are 5/10, 5/10, and 2/10 satisfied! In other words, not satisfied at all. How satisfied with the financial remunerations are the leaders/owners? They are 8/10 and 7/10 satisfied. In other words, pretty satisfied, though doubtless still wanting more. Clearly, the business is making money, which it is, but the rewards are going to the owners. Thus, the higher motivational levels of the leaders/owners are not really so significant since its source is largely monetary, which they control.

And the monetary control and acquisition can lead into other motivational areas too: it is probably significant that Louise is 8/10 satisfied with her top motivator, Defender, since that means security. It is highly likely that remunerating oneself sufficiently promotes high feelings of security too. Note here that her third motivator, Searcher, is only 'OK' at 6/10.

Here, for now then, we have a final point to make: both Louise and Theo have conflicting top motivators. For Louise it is the Defender/Searcher in the top three; for Theo it is the Spirit/Director, which we have commented on before. The point about this is that although conflicts in motivators can be productive, giving, for example, someone a dual perspective on situations, they can also be extremely stymying: indecision and procrastination can result from motivators pulling in different directions. In Louise's case this can be in the area of going for change (Searcher, making a difference) and yet actively seeking to resist it (Defender, security and maintaining the status quo). Further, especially with Theo's Spirit (I am free) and Director (but I manage you) motivators, it is easy for him to appear inconsistent with staff and even failing to walk the talk: as in staff perceiving Theo saying one thing, but the rules not applying to him.

Before we come to the vital issue of what to do about all of this, let us now extend what we did in Figure 1.5 to all the PMA scores for all the motivators. What does that look like?

						Average per motivator
Spirit	3	5	2	7	6	5
Builder	8	5	5	2	7	5
Defender	8	7	5			7
Searcher	6	4				5
Expert	7					7
Creator	5	7				6
Friend	4					4
Director	6	8				7
Star		not in anyone's top 3				n/a

Figure 1.6 PMA score patterns for BoL

Activity 1.6

From this Figure 1.6 you will clearly see that Spirit and Builder are far and away the two most important motivators driving this group/team/company. However, it is always good to review the 'non-motivators' as it were, and see if any issues might arise. The three most important low motivators here are: Star, which is in no-one's profile and scores significantly lower than any other motivator, Friend and Expert, which have only one person each who have it in their top three profile. What issues might these low motivators suggest for the functioning of the team?

Indeed, there are some very important points to make as a result of what seem inconsequentially low motivators. Are they that important? After the work of Hertzberg, we call these 'hygiene factors'.[12] Another way of explaining them would be as Achilles' heels: weaknesses that can trip you up if you don't pay attention to them, and finally, as in the actual case of Achilles, kill you – your team's productivity, your business – if the heel becomes exposed.[13]

Take Star, then, the most obvious and seemingly irrelevant motivator to this 'team'. Could this possibly have any adverse effects in the functioning of the group/team? Surprisingly, yes! And this is to do with the remit or purpose of the company. We always have to, with Maps, consider the context. It is not enough to say that a very low Star motivator in any team is going to be a problem, for that would not be true. But in this case we have to ask, what does this team actually do? What is their remit?

Their remit is to create web pages for clients who wish to ...? To what?

Activity 1.7

Think about this carefully before reading on. What do most clients wish to do when they commission a web company to create their site and pages for them? If you have a website, what do you wish and hope it will do for you or your organisation?

They wish to stand out, they wish to be noticed on the internet, they almost invariably want to be found and for their particular offering – whatever it is – to be attractive, to be compelling, and to convert browsers into leads and ultimately paying customers. In short, one aspect of creating web pages is understanding how to make clients shine – that is, to star!! But if you have nothing in your own (team) drive or energies or motivations that identifies with that 'feeling', then it is more likely that you are going to be creating functional websites, but not 'starring' ones. You may have the technology and the templates through which to create something for your clients, but you do not have the feeling, the desire, for how this might look in a way that might more deeply satisfy them.

Now this point needs qualifying. For there will be clients whose own Star motivator is low and whose expectations are purely functional, and so the kind of work that BoL does is likely to be sufficient or some might say, 'good enough'. However, for the more ambitious, more demanding, more market-savvy kind of client, there will be a real problem emerging somewhere down the line. And indeed, this is exactly what occurred and was reflected in the high churn-rate of clients; conversely, this also meant that what the company/team motivators actually were – that is, very sales-orientated – was constantly in play and being exercised. The company was quite brilliant at bringing large numbers of new clients on board, but then far less good at retaining them.

A final, and advanced point, here is that the Star is a relationship driven motivator: it requires other people for it to be fully realised. It also requires a certain level of quality interaction with one's 'self' ('self' here understood as referring to an individual or a team or an organisation). So, for example, on an individual level, the Star motivated person may spend a lot of time seeking to impress others, and the most immediate and obvious way of doing this is via how one appears – clothes, accoutrements, knick-knacks, make-up, grooming and so on and so forth. But Star motivated teams do the same: they forge a specific look and identity, and this differentiates them. This 'identity' becomes attractive to others, since it is invariably (when successful and well-thought through) successful. There is, then, in the Star motivator a self-concern that can be positively beneficial not only to clients but to employees as well: it's a sense in which employees and clients alike get lots of specific 'strokes' (this is a metaphor, but think cats) that turns them on![14]

To have such a low Star motivator for the team profile is, then, to run a triple risk: that no-one is interested in allowing others within the team to

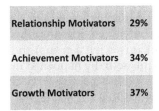

Relationship Motivators	29%
Achievement Motivators	34%
Growth Motivators	37%

Figure 1.7 RAG scores for BoL

shine; and also to appear as a somewhat (to use the word as a metaphor) 'dowdy' group who take little interest in how they present themselves. And additionally, if the purpose of websites be to make one's clients appear sensational, fabulous, or some other strong 'star' word, then it is highly likely that this component of the remit will fall far short. Phew! These are all serious issues for the longevity of the company.

More briefly, we have two other 'low' motivators in this team mix: The Friend and the Expert. Picking up on the theme of Relationship motivators (of which Star is one), Friend too is Relationship driven. If we look at the RAG score[15] for the team we find: 29–34–37.

In other words (see Figure 1.7) Relationship forming and sustaining is the least important set of motivators for this group. Indeed, Friend being low is a polarity reinforcement of Spirit being high: there is tension between wanting to belong and wanting to be autonomous. Clearly, here – aside from the work – there is little connecting the team members. Because this is low, the leader and senior team need to make a special effort to prevent team fragmentation and disintegration, which in this case will manifest itself as high staff turnover. Coming back to our model, this means that interdependence is unlikely, and independence will be far more to the fore.

Finally, it is slightly concerning that Expert is not in the top four. Virtually every other IT company we have mapped has Expert somewhere in the top three; the fact is that computer programmers tend to be by their very nature somewhat 'geeky' and into coding and their specialisms, classic signs of the expert. Expert is fifth in the rankings, but this is only because one member, Max, has it as a spike[16] at 30/40. If his score were only 20 or even 10, then the whole ranking of fifth would quite dramatically change. The good thing is that he is 7/10 satisfied with his current expertise and learning, but how is learning disseminated and promoted within a company like this? The key point that arises from this deliberation is simply this: how can the remit of the company – to create effective websites for their clients – really be serviced if the learning levels, the expertise, is low? And indeed, down the line, this did have important consequences for the company.

Activity 1.8

I discussed earlier about addressing issues and we now come to that point. What would you recommend as activities that this team/company might do to strengthen its teamwork (given it is a group) and to become more successful? Also, what do you think actually happened in this case study?

What is vital now is to establish a core part of the Motivational Mapping process; the part that is called Reward Strategies. We have covered some of this in earlier books,[17] but since we are now talking about top performing teams, it is vital that we cover this in even more detail. It is important to stress, too, that Reward Strategies, as a process, cannot be applied mechanically: no one 'reward' will work in all situations at all times. Furthermore, keep in mind that there are rewards for individuals, for teams, and for whole organisations, and these are quite distinct. Our book, *Mapping Motivation for Coaching*, clearly had a focus on individuals; here we consider rewards which are more appropriate for the team (noting, of course, this particular team is the whole company).

The Motivational Team Map itself provides automated ideas in its output. Five suggestions are made for the top motivator, and then three each for the second and third motivators in the team's profile. This looks like the information in Figure 1.8 where we have the recommendations for BoL's top motivator.

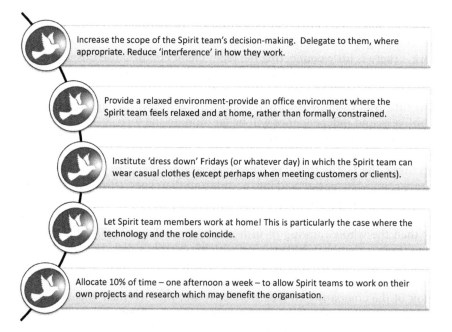

Increase the scope of the Spirit team's decision-making. Delegate to them, where appropriate. Reduce 'interference' in how they work.

Provide a relaxed environment-provide an office environment where the Spirit team feels relaxed and at home, rather than formally constrained.

Institute 'dress down' Fridays (or whatever day) in which the Spirit team can wear casual clothes (except perhaps when meeting customers or clients).

Let Spirit team members work at home! This is particularly the case where the technology and the role coincide.

Allocate 10% of time – one afternoon a week – to allow Spirit teams to work on their own projects and research which may benefit the organisation.

Figure 1.8 Team Map Reward Strategies for Spirit as top motivator

Clearly, these recommendations – along with the ones for Builder and Defender in the case of BoL – need to be considered as a starting point for further examination. They are particularly geared around immediate and practical advice to the leader of this team, but they are also brief headlines that will need some expansion if they are to be implemented. Finally, because this team is the whole company, it is highly probable, as in fact happened, that the Reward Strategies needed also to include organisational level rewards.

Finally, the effective consultant here will bring in the hygiene factor of the Star motivator. This will not be something anybody within the team is motivated to want to do. But the entrée is by way of connecting it to a motivator they do want: namely, the Builder. What if, one might say, this company stood out – developed one or two unique aspects that differentiated it from others – what would that do to sales? Using some example of a competitor type company that seems to be extremely successful financially, and is not too close to home, might well spur the owners to want to up their game.[18] Also, check the Resources Section for team ideas for the Star motivator to see if any of these appear applicable in the circumstance of your low Star team!

Notes

1 James Sale, *Mapping Motivation* (Gower/Routledge, 2016), Chapter 6.
2 There is also more team information in Chapters 5 and 6 of *Mapping Motivation for Leadership*, James Sale and Jane Thomas (Routledge, 2019).
3 Evan Wittenberg, director of the Wharton Graduate Leadership Program, notes that team size is 'not necessarily an issue people think about immediately, but it is important'. According to Wittenberg, while the research on optimal team numbers is 'not conclusive, it does tend to fall into the five to 12 range, though some say five to nine is best, and the number six has come up a few times' – https://whr.tn/2ZSUzX0
4 This number also has a sort of 'divine' endorsement in that Jesus Christ had twelve disciples, which was his team that changed the world.
5 Ringelmann's famous study on pulling a rope – often called the Ringelmann effect – analysed people alone and in groups as they pulled on a rope. Ringelmann then measured the pull force. As he added more and more people to the rope, Ringelmann discovered that the total force generated by the group rose, but the average force exerted by each group member declined, thereby discrediting the theory that a group team effort results in increased effort. Ringelmann attributed this to what was then called 'social loafing' – a condition where a group or team tends to 'hide' the lack of individual effort – https://whr.tn/2ZSUzX0
6 There are four quadrants of motivation, which we define as the Optimal Zone (80–100% motivated), the Boost Zone (60–79%), the Risk Zone (35–59%) and the Action Zone (below 35% motivated). 35–60–80 are the crossover points. Below 60% is a cause for real concern. For more detailed information about these Zones, see *Mapping Motivation*, ibid., Chapter 4. Also, go to Figure 2.1 in this book.
7 For more on polarity reinforcement see *Mapping Motivation for Coaching*, James Sale and Bevis Moynan (Routledge, 2018), Chapter 6, and also *Mapping Motivation*, ibid., Chapter 4. Also see, *Mapping Motivation for Leadership*, ibid.

8 For more on this see *Mapping Motivation for Leadership*, ibid., Chapter 6. This is not to say that Spirit motivators cannot be good team players, but their deployment needs to be carefully assessed since they do not wish to belong by definition!

9 For more on the correlation between motivation and performance and productivity, see *Mapping Motivation*, ibid., Chapter 5, *Mapping Motivation for Coaching*, ibid., Chapter 3, and *Mapping Motivation for Engagement*, ibid., Chapter 1.

10 Personal and company names have all been anonymised of course to preserve confidentiality; and to repeat – we are not discussing 'success' stories, but real-life teams where even small improvements can be highly significant.

11 The actual number is 4.6, which is rounded up here to create a whole number.

12 Frederick Herzberg, *The Motivation to Work* (Wiley, 1959). See *Mapping Motivation*, ibid., Chapter 4 for more on this.

13 According to Greek legends, Achilles was invulnerable because his mother dipped his body into the river Styx (one of the four rivers of hell or Hades) shortly after he was born. This dousing in the immortal waters made him invulnerable to any weapon, but where she held him in the water – by his heel – remained dry and so was his weak spot. The Trojan Paris, guided by the archer god, Apollo, thus killed Achilles by shooting an arrow at that one weak spot.

14 Strokes is a technical term from Transactional Analysis. People who are Relationship-type motivated are always thinking, 'How do I get strokes round here?'. For more on this go to *Motivational Mapping*, ibid., Chapter 3. Also, see *Games People Play*, Eric Berne (Andre Deutsch, 1966).

15 The RAG score is included in every Motivational Map. It stands for the relative percentage scores of the Relationship–Achievement–Growth motivators.

16 Spike and inverse spike are technical terms we use to describe either very high or low Motivational Map scores. So a score of 30 or above for a motivator means that this motivator is particularly strong – a real focus or craving; whereas a score of 10 or less, an inverse spike, means the motivator is weak and not attractive or compelling at all. Several examples of spikes and inverse spikes are covered in *Mapping Motivation for Leadership*, ibid.

17 *Mapping Motivation*, ibid., *Mapping Motivation for Coaching*, ibid., *Mapping Motivation for Leadership*, ibid., especially.

18 In terms of outcomes, the Mapping process had a profound effect and the company is still in business: the most important change being the switch in its sales and marketing focus. It identified its narrower niche and began exclusively to market itself to sole traders or very small companies who did not require deep expertise, but only a basic web page to get going. Thus, as they ditched their larger, more demanding, and more 'Star' requirement type clients, they gained momentum. The Maps had opened up the idea that they pile it high and sell it cheap, and that way was the route to profitability. The Maps, effectively, helped them identify the correct strategy for their business.

Chapter 2

Reward Strategies

In Chapter 1 we looked at the four properties of a team, and also whether a team Map might indicate, without having to look any further afield, whether a group of people really were a team or simply just that, a group. The answer is yes; Motivational Maps can quite clearly show whether a group of people is functioning as a team or not. Clearly, this is very valuable. For one thing, from a consultancy, training or coaching perspective, an external support agency can almost immediately get a handle on some of the issues that are besetting a particular group within an organisation. Furthermore, internally an organisation might well suspect or know that a particular group or 'team' or department is not functioning as a team, but be unclear as to the reasons why. Here the Motivational Map, as we saw with BoL, can be very specific. Finally, and really surprisingly (though not perhaps when you really think about it), the Motivational Map can uncover problems that the parent organisation was not even aware of![1] Because they were not aware of the problems does not mean that the problems were trivial; on the contrary, the Maps can expose some serious issues that were, consciously or otherwise, hidden or below the surface. This was certainly the case with BoL.

However, we need to consider the wider issue of rewards. This is a theme we will be coming back to because it is so important. The Resources section contains a chart in which seven team rewards are identified for each of the nine motivators; this means we have or are offering some 63 targeted ideas for consultants and managers to use with their teams. But to be clear, there are many more than that; indeed, there are hundreds, if not thousands, of possible rewards that we might offer teams. The key thing for consultants and managers to do is to reflect on the meanings of each motivator, as in asking 'what would this motivator being fulfilled actually look like?' and then to ask themselves: so what would I need to do to achieve it?

Motivational Mapping calls this handling of rewards our 'Reward Strategies'[2] process. As our previous books[3] have made plain, the first thing to understand about rewards is that they are intrinsically linked to our performance in all walks of life, including work. We learn at an early age that if we do the 'right' thing – that is, we perform appropriately – we get rewarded. Our parents and carers first train us in this methodology, but it goes on ever afterwards as part of the socialisation we experience: at school there are gold stars, high marks, unique dispensations, special honours, and praise itself that we can garner if – big *if* – we behave and perform properly. At college and then work, the same principles apply: perform and get rewarded. Finally, the ultimate 'honours' of this world[4] are bestowed on those who are perceived to have made the biggest contribution to human welfare or to the well-being of their own communities; but necessarily these biggest contributions mean we have sustained our performance throughout and over a long period of time. Indeed, we could almost agree with Liz Ryan[5] when she states that, 'The truth is, you don't need motivation programmes to motivate people', for if we rewarded them properly the 'programmes' really would be unnecessary!

Activity 2.1

How many levels of performance are there? Clue: re-read the Summary of Motivational Maps section. And why are there this number of levels?

Because, as the Summary makes clear, there are four levels of motivation, then there must be four levels of performance, since motivation drives performance and is correlated with it. So, there are four 'real' or meaningful levels of performance, although that does not prevent individuals or organisations establishing less of more levels. Thus, we can obviously contemplate two levels: good or bad; three levels: high–average–low; or we can consider five levels: excellent–good–average–weak–poor, and so on. Indeed, we can have seven or ten levels if we choose, and a scoring out of ten is a frequent phenomenon that we encounter in organisations. But the reality is that four levels corresponds to the workings of the Pareto Principle,[6] which is 80/20 or 4:1.

This is important to grasp for a number of reasons, the most important of which is that it gives us an intuitive understanding of what the 'levels' – or the numbers – mean. If we were to say, for example, that there are ten levels, then what would it mean, verbally, to be at level 3? We could write out definitions for all ten levels, but this would be difficult to keep in mind at all times, since it would be more complicated than remembering a ten-digit telephone number!

On the other hand, too few produces too simplistic a rating. With three levels, for example – high–average–low – we do not really have enough range. But with four it is easy to create memorable designations and furthermore it avoids having an odd number, which is important as it circumvents the opportunity for managers to rate everybody exactly in the middle! A sort of comfortable, non-committal kind of rating. An even number of levels requires a more decisive interpretation of how someone is doing.

Level	Motivation	Map Zone	Performance
4	80-100%	Optimal	Outstanding
3	60-79%	Boost	Excellent
2	35-59%	Risk	Good
1	10-34%	Action	Poor
0	x	-	NO

Figure 2.1 Motivation and performance: four levels or zones

In terms of wording, our preferred terminology is: Outstanding–Excellent–Good–Poor.

Activity 2.2

We have said that there are four levels or zones of motivation and performance, but looking at Figure 2.1 there appear to be five! The bottom row of the chart, and which is separated by a thick black line, seems to be another level or zone. Why do you think this is? What explanation might there be for saying there are not five levels or zones, but four, plus 0 (4+0)?[7] What is '+0'?

The reason quite simply is that zero is not a number or level; the absence of motivation, of skill, of performance, is precisely that: an absence, a nil.[8] Thus we refer to the levels or zones as '4+0', aware that the '+0' is not a level at all.[9]

So the question we have to ask ourselves from the Reward Strategies perspective is how, typically, people are rewarded for their performances? Keep in mind, they are not – *we are not* – rewarded generally – for our high motivation levels. Motivation is – in sales-speak[10] – a feature; but we are rewarded for performance, which is the benefit that occurs most frequently when the motivation levels are high. This applies individually and for each team. If teams are not rewarded appropriately, then they will cease performing over time.

Activity 2.3

Most would agree that at level 0 – no performance at all – the rewards are likely to be zero too, or even punishment. Certainly, no-one can survive long in an organisation without performing at some level.[11] But consider level 1, what we are calling a poor performance level,[12] what rewards do organisations typically award poor performance? And your answer needs

Level	Performance	Rewards
4	Outstanding	
3	Excellent	
2	Good	
1	Poor	
0		

Figure 2.2 Performance and rewards

to be framed in the terminology of the performance levels themselves: so, does poor performance generate 0, poor, good, excellent or outstanding rewards? When you have done that, consider good, excellent and outstanding performance; what level of rewards do they each generate, defined using the same terminology?

The most common answer to the question what do you get if you perform poorly is: you receive poor rewards! In other words, the rewards are commensurate to the performance, and that does seem sensible[13] – at least until you really look at it and what happens in the world of work and in life more generally. So, equally, too, people think that if they perform 'good' (grammatically, that is, well) they will receive 'good' rewards; excellent performance generates excellent rewards; and outstanding performance creates the icing on the cake, namely outstanding rewards. This all seems fair and right, because there is a kind of parity between the performance and the rewards. But this ignores the startling fact that no-one really finds the world full of parity, fairness and just rewards! Indeed, we are always complaining of, and observing, the exact opposite. What really, then, is going on?

The reality is that poor performance actually produces no rewards or zero; we drop below the think black horizontal line in Figure 2.2. Indeed, all organisations, except the most dysfunctional (which are therefore on the tipping point of collapse), seek to remove or, if they cannot, to mitigate poor employee performance. And this is true of poorly performing teams as well. The most obvious methodologies for dealing with poorly performing teams is, firstly, to appoint a new leader, or secondly, to reconstitute the team, changing personnel, removing certain individuals and bringing in fresh blood (see Chapter 6 for more on recruitment). Thus, in a sense, poor performance is like no performance in that the rewards are the same: that is, there are no rewards! The major difference really is that there are far more poor performers than no-performers, because even a moderately random selection process[14] usually weeds out those who have absolutely no skills or aptitude to perform in the area necessary for the organisation's future. The idea of changing personnel in a team, of course, is precisely what Motivational Maps can help enable far more effectively than simply considering skill sets. However, we need to keep in mind that whereas new leadership or a change of team personnel may be the automatic default methodology for dealing with poor performance, the review of appropriate Reward Strategies may be the third and, in the long run, most effective solution.

But to return to Activity 2.3, if poor performance receives no reward, what about a 'good' performance? This is perhaps the trickiest level to answer, for we need to understand something highly counterintuitive. Namely, that a 'good performance' really means something quite different! So, the answer is: a good performance usually produces a poor reward! Yes, awful and as unfair as it sounds, this is the situation that the vast majority of individuals and teams encounter on a daily, weekly and annual basis. The reason for this is to understand what 'good' here means: it actually means 'average' performance.[15] It means doing the job – getting the job done, which is 'good', but that is all. Hence, when bosses come to consider rewards for their teams and staff, they reflect that they are paying X to do Y, and X has actually done Y; a good performance, but there is nothing 'extra' about it, so why would one need to reward any person or team for 'just doing their job'? And this, of course, is why so many staff feel underappreciated: 'I am doing a good job' they cry. Why yes, they are; but they are being paid for it. Why give more? In a sense doing the job is 'good' but it is also 'average', and even 'mediocre'. Nothing distinguishes the performance.

To fully understand the import of the above paragraph is to begin to understand why there is an epidemic of complaints about management, and a worldwide situation in which disengagement and demotivation are rife.[16] People and teams rarely feel that their efforts are being appreciated; but on the other side of the coin, not enough managers are providing an environment in which 'going the extra mile', seeking to contribute in a way that exceeds the contractual arrangement,[17] is made sufficiently clear or even inviting. There are, as might be expected, problems in doing so, since what we are suggesting in a way seems to be a license for bosses to exploit staff and their teams: to wit, whatever your contractual role is, we expect you to go far beyond it. This, then, can create a new 'norm' of performance, which itself becomes the 'average' and staff and teams can get locked into a spiral of performance that can lead to burnout. However, that does not obviate the need for individuals and teams to outperform, since doing so is not only good from a career and monetary perspective,[18] but actually is also intrinsic to high levels of self-esteem. In other words, feeling good about ourselves. Furthermore, let's keep in mind David Kolb's observation[19]: 'A company staffed by "cheated" individuals who expect far more than they get is headed for trouble'.

Figure 2.3 Performance and reward pattern

Thus, 'good' performance leads to poor rewards; furthermore, excellent performance only leads to 'good' rewards. We regularly see this latter phenomenon in action too. The individual or team performing at an excellent level – going way above their job description(s) – sometimes being the mainstay of an organisation's overall success. But then, after 1 or 3 or 5 or 7 years, they become increasingly aware that their rewards are 'good' but, given their contribution, insufficient. If they stay in post, they begin to experience burnout, as the mismatch between performance and reward creates a form of cognitive dissonance. If they are a team, then the turnover starts to accelerate: organisations start shedding their excellent performers, and the scramble begins to recruit anew and do the same thing all over again.

Before coming to the outstanding performance, perhaps you may have noticed a pattern?

Activity 2.4

What is the pattern you notice in Figure 2.3? Given you have correctly identified it, revisit your answer to Activity 2.3 and what are the rewards for outstanding performance? Give your final answer to this question: what sort of rewards do you get when you are an outstanding performer?

The pattern is, of course, that rewards lag the performance by one level[20]: poor performance gets nothing, good performance gets poor rewards, and excellent performance only achieves good rewards.

But at the top, outstanding performance does not get excellent rewards, for here the model flips. For outstanding performance gets outstanding rewards, or perhaps more dramatically, outstanding performers get it 'all'. In other words, they receive a massively disproportionate share of the spoils: the lionesses and junior lions may get their dinner, but not before the king lion – or top dog[21] (to mix animals if not metaphors)! – takes his or her pick of what, and all, he or she wants. We see this in virtually every sporting match or competition we ever watch: the outstanding performer, the winner, who may win only 'by a nose'[22,] still takes not only most of the money, but the acknowledgement, acclaim and recognition too.[23]

Hence, if we but knew it, we all want to be outstanding performers because that's where the real, full rewards are. And if we are a team, then we need to appreciate that fact, and also understand both the four criteria that enable teams to function at an optimum level and the importance of motivation overall.

But saying all that, there is something else to understand about these four levels of performance and reward.

Activity 2.5

If we ask ourselves the question, what is the gap between poor performance and good performance, what would your answer be? To answer this question, consider some skill that it may be necessary to perform: say, speaking French, or writing software programs, or understanding financial spreadsheets, or speaking in public, and so on and so forth. Imagine in any one of these, you perform 'poorly' – how big a gap is it to perform well (aka, good)? Is it a small step? A substantial step? A large step? Or a very large step?

Clearly, this is not an exact science and in any case may vary from skill type to skill type; for example, some micro-skills may be relatively easy to improve upon in a short space of time. But for any significant skill set, there is probably at least a large step to undertake before our level of performance shifts upwards. Thus, we would say that to move from a poor level of performance to a good level is a significant or large jump. Similarly, to move from being good to being excellent is also a large manoeuvre. Equally, we would say that to move from no performance level at all to a poor level is a large jump.

So the movements look like Figure 2.4.

As we review this, we notice that at the final and top level of performance – the level of being outstanding – we have a question mark. Why is that? Is it because the stretch from Excellent to Outstanding is not a large jump, but perhaps a very large jump, which is why so few attain it?[24]

Actually, the exact opposite is the case: the difference between an Excellent and an Outstanding performance is very small, or a small step, in terms of the performance (though not of course in terms of the rewards), and the clue to understanding how one transitions from one to the other is contained

Figure 2.4 The stretch of performance levels

in the wording: the outstanding performer and the outstanding team (as with the outstanding organisation) not only performs at an excellent level but also 'out-stands' or, to give it its full etymological significance, 'stands out'. This 'standing out' is, as it were, something not strictly always part of the performance itself[25] – though it does enhance it – but more a communication's job, a Public Relations (PR) type of messaging for oneself or for the team, as one undertakes to achieve a specific result or objective; for in the end, all performance is geared round achieving a specific outcome. In other words, outstanding performance is most frequently seen where performers direct attention to their own excellent performance, and this itself boosts the performance!

How is this possible? On the one – and cynical – hand we have all observed the employees in organisations who draw attention to themselves and 'big up' their performance, often at the expense of others; and these usually have to move on quickly before their absence of results finally catches up with them. So this type of apparent or false performance is not what we are talking about here. But rather we have in mind the kind of performance that starts with what Virgil[26] observed some 2000 years ago: 'Success nourished them; they seemed to be able, and so they were able'.

Success nourished them – they saw what they could do, they believed (see more on belief in Chapter 7) in what they could do, and this became empowering for further achievement. And this 'success' is a form of visible demonstration – a PR to themselves as it were, as well as to the world. Notice that the quotation is referring to not just the individual but to 'they', a team, and furthermore that this links back to our point about the importance of 'belief' within teams: this becomes effectively a tangible force or power that others can see and feel.

Also, we need to realise that this belief goes back to the motivational triangle; for belief fuels motivation, which is the energy necessary to perform.

We know that performance derives from the confluence or combination of direction, skills and motivation,[27] so that motivation directly impacts the ability to perform. But in Figure 2.5 we see the three sources of motivation itself within the human psyche, and we are reminded that beliefs about the self (and here we can add, beliefs about the team from within and without) and about the future (expectations) are crucial for high energy and emotional drive. In mentioning 'without' we are of course going beyond merely the team's perception of itself to others' perception of the team: this is where the expectation of others drives higher levels of performance (for example, high parental expectations create high performing children) and also create an internal pressure to do even better, to achieve even more, until at the very top end of performance many others cannot compete against you (or the team) because your reputation precedes you and intimidates others. We see this in sport all the time. Until their bubble bursts, the top performers seem unstoppable.

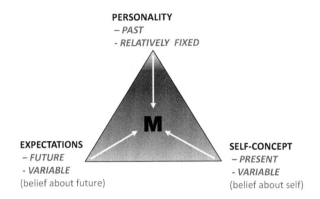

Figure 2.5 Three sources of motivation

Putting this all together, then, we have Figure 2.6 where we consider how the performance and reward levels correlate. What is most important to understand here is that if we wish to get beyond the point where our staff feel 'cheated', we have to 'over-reward', which, if we understand Motivational Mapping, is not the same thing as 'overpaying'[28] them. But we have to get into what might be termed the 'majority' mind-set – the mind-set of the 'good' performers, meaning average, which will be the majority of employees, especially in larger organisations – and see that the poor rewards that they typically receive are never going to get them to move to another level. On the contrary, poor rewards are going to encourage them to do less, to obstruct or sabotage, or to move employment elsewhere.

We need, then, to over-reward if we are to have any chance of obtaining superior performance from our employees and our teams. To be clear, research indicates[29] that when employees feel totally rewarded and engaged then their performance and productivity is likely to be higher. Notice the word 'totally' – this circumvents the ubiquitous sense of never being rewarded enough, and also that resentment which is bred through the perception that only the 'outstanding' star performers are ever really being rewarded.

Activity 2.6

Before going any further, then, what might 'over-rewarding' look like to you? How might one over-reward a member of staff, or a particular team? What specifically would you do or give to someone or some team you wanted to 'over-reward'? Think about this as widely as possible: what might the tangible rewards be, and what intangible rewards might be important?

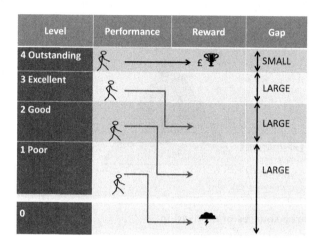

Figure 2.6 Four levels of performance and reward

Keeping in mind our model in Figure 2.6, we now need an overview of how a typically total rewards model might appear. A good example is from the work of leading consultant Duncan Brown.[30] Brown observes that

> many [organisations] talk about total rewards yet do little beyond copying what other employers are doing and, perhaps, introducing flexible benefits plans to make employees feel well recognised, rewarded and engaged. Indeed, some employers may even have used total rewards terminology to disguise cost savings, pay restraint, benefits cut and reductions in their total reward costs .... This helps to explain the growing divorce between productivity and real wage growth.

Do little beyond copying? Disguising cost savings? And perhaps explaining the absence of increased productivity[31] as real wages grow? This is a pretty bleak picture. Duncan advocates– with the interaction of financial and non-financial factors – tailoring an approach for each individual organisation, and not to develop a 'single pay practice'. His total rewards model is useful.

This model, of course, takes no account of actual motivational factors, except in the familiar and, we think, simplistic idea that there are intrinsic and extrinsic motivators. Motivational Maps, by way of contrast, regards all motivators as intrinsic: base cash is a motivator, and we call it the Builder motivator. But as we have pointed out before: at a certain and low level people work not for their motivators, but to suffice their needs – they need cash to survive, and so at that level the idea that their 'real' motivators might be met is not really an option. The kind of work where this

	Common Example	Reward Elements	Definition
INTRINSIC Elements which contribute to internal value or motivation	Quality of work	**Engagement factors**	**TOTAL REWARD**
	Work/life balance		
	Inspiration/values		
	Enabling environment		
	Growth/opportunity		
EXTRINISIC All the things to which we can assign a monetary value	Tangible benefits eg cars, professional membership, discount	**Active benefits**	**TOTAL REMUNERATION**
	Retirement	**Passive benefits**	
	Health and welfare		
	Holidays		
	Stock/equity	**Long-term rewards/incentives**	**TOTAL DIRECT COMPENSATION**
	Performance shares		
	Annual incentive	**Short-term variable**	
	Bonus/split awards		
	Team awards		**TOTAL CASH**
	Base salary	**Base cash**	
	Hourly wages		

Figure 2.7 Duncan Brown's total rewards model

principle applies will be low grade, low skill and usually a non-professional type of activity. To discuss these situations here is inappropriate for there is little to discuss, since the Map motivators will not apply in the usual way: clearly, what subsistence workers require is their 'daily bread' so that they can continue to subsist! Their needs need to be met, full stop. Whether an employer or organisation chooses to do that is outside the remit of this book, except to say that the 'labourer is worthy of their hire[32]' and so should be paid fairly.

So let us take this model in Figure 2.7 and superimpose on it the Map motivators and we find Figure 2.8.

Note that varying motivators occur in each of the three sections, the full RAG spectrum is only in the Achievement section, probably because performance is most geared to 'achievement'.

This model, I think, more accurately develops what Duncan Brown is really seeking to achieve, especially when he writes that employers need to:

1. *Research the drivers and determinants of their own employees' engagement levels;*
2. *Explore how rewards can and could influence their engagement levels;*

Common Example	Reward Elements	Motivators	Type
Quality of work	Engagement factors	Searcher	Growth Achievement
Work/life balance		Spirit	
Inspiration/values		Creator	
Enabling environment		Expert	
Growth/opportunity		Director	
Tangible benefits eg cars, professional membership, discount	Active benefits	Expert Defender Creator	Relationship Achievement Growth
Retirement	Passive benefits		
Health and welfare			
Holidays			
Stock/equity	Short and long term money	Star Defender Friend Builder	Achievement Relationship
Performance shares			
Annual incentive			
Bonus/split awards			
Team awards			
Base salary			
Hourly wages			

Figure 2.8 Total rewards and Motivational Maps

3. *Give employees some options and choices to tailor their own packages where possible; and*
4. *Train managers to communicate about reward and ensure that practical implementation matches policy intention.*

The drivers and determinants are simply their Motivational Map profiles; the exploration of rewards and the options and choices are what we are considering in Figures 2.7 and 2.8; and training managers to communicate this, is the follow-through.

Employers, then, are perhaps misdirected as they get their HR departments (or is that teams?) trying to create a one-size-fits-all 'best Reward Strategies practice'. Of course, it's important that whatever is developed is fair and affordable; but critically, what this is suggesting is the importance of flexibility.

Also, we note that at the base of the Reward Strategies stands the Builder motivator, not the Defender in the usual Maslow type configuration. And this of course kicks in because, although the employees are not working for their daily bread and are beyond subsistence level, the salary – wages – need to be *enough*. Hence, at this point, the money – Builder motivator – is foundational. And this corresponds to the 'common sense' view that many

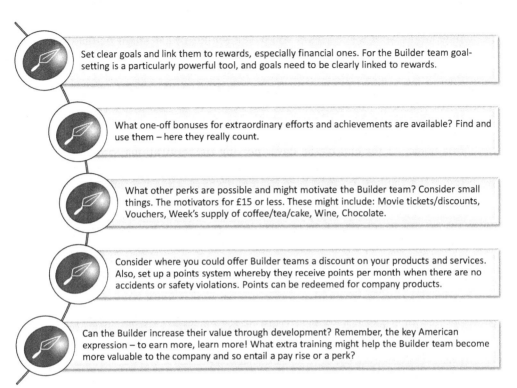

Set clear goals and link them to rewards, especially financial ones. For the Builder team goal-setting is a particularly powerful tool, and goals need to be clearly linked to rewards.

What one-off bonuses for extraordinary efforts and achievements are available? Find and use them – here they really count.

What other perks are possible and might motivate the Builder team? Consider small things. The motivators for £15 or less. These might include: Movie tickets/discounts, Vouchers, Week's supply of coffee/tea/cake, Wine, Chocolate.

Consider where you could offer Builder teams a discount on your products and services. Also, set up a points system whereby they receive points per month when there are no accidents or safety violations. Points can be redeemed for company products.

Can the Builder increase their value through development? Remember, the key American expression – to earn more, learn more! What extra training might help the Builder team become more valuable to the company and so entail a pay rise or a perk?

Figure 2.9 Five team rewards for Builder motivator

business owners and executives[33] consider that it is only about the money. Clearly, it is not, but we have to take it into account in a Reward Strategies package.

Activity 2.7

Since this book is about top performing teams, what might be the 'team awards' (see Figures 2.7 and 2.8) we could make at the Builder level?[34] What ideas do you have that might reward a Builder orientated team?

The full repertoire of Team Rewards for all nine motivators is to be found in the Resources section of this book. But in order to conclude this chapter with one set of examples – and a foundational one – let's look at five ideas for motivating a Builder Team.

Activity 2.8

Consider a team that you have either been in or know that is particularly commercially – or Builder – orientated; in other words, in your opinion, they are heavily motivated by money. Study Figure 2.9. Choose the best three motivational ideas contained in the figure and explain why you think they might work for the team you have in mind. What might be the draw-backs, reservations or issues that might occur?

What we have done in Figure 2.9, of course, can be carried out with the other team motivational rewards that we list in the Resources section. The key thing is to be sure what the team's actual motivators are; and here the Motivational Map is indispensable.

Keep in mind the whole idea of Reward Strategies as we progress through this book. At the end of the day, knowing the motivational profile is not enough in and of itself. We have to know what the triggers are that are go-ing to get the best performance from employees. Even if I fail to mention Reward Strategies in some particular context, since I may be focusing on some other issue, make sure you always consider it. Remember, we are con-ditioned from childhood to work for rewards we want.

In the next chapter we move on to addressing the first of the four charac-teristics of a top performing teams: The Remit, part 1!

Notes

1 According to Sydney Yoshida, 'The Iceberg of Ignorance, Quality Improvement and TQM at Calsonic in Japan and Overseas' (1989), the top executives are only aware of 4% of the problems, the team managers of 9%, the team leaders of 74% and the staff of 100%! – https://bit.ly/2DNPae5

2 According to John Bratton and Jeff Gold, 'Reward system refers to all the mon-etary, non-monetary and psychological payments that an organisation provides for its employees in exchange for the work they perform'. In Bratton and Gold, *Human Resource Management Theory and Practice*, 4th edition, Chapter 10 (Palgrave Macmillan, 2007). It's the whole 'package' in other words.

3 See *Mapping Motivation*, James Sale (Routledge, 2016), Chapter 5; *Mapping Mo-tivation for Coaching*, James Sale and Bevis Moynan (Routledge, 2018), Chapter 3; *Mapping Motivation for Engagement*, James Sale and Steve Jones (Routledge, 2019), Chapter 1.

4 Whether this be becoming the CEO of a large multinational corporation, the President of a country or institution, receiving an honour from the Queen or in-ternational committee, winning the Nobel Prize or any other major award, or at local level being Secretary of a local club, and so on. These titles become badges of honour. Then there are the medals, cups, trophies, certificates and suchlike that all can win at any age.

5 Liz Ryan, Linkedin's Pulse Blog, cited in *MoneyWeek*, 27/5/2016.

6 For more on the Pareto Principle, see our *Mapping Motivation*, ibid. and *Map-ping Motivation for Coaching*, ibid. Also, for a definitive text on its overall appli-cations, see Richard Koch, *The 80/20 Principle* (Nicholas Brealey, 1997).

7 For experienced Motivational Mappers and alert readers of all our books in this series, this '4+1' formula may come as no surprise. We introduced such a concept as it applied to leadership in *Mapping Motivation*, ibid., and as well as expanding it in, *Mapping Motivation for Leadership*, ibid. In the leadership case it was because we argued that leadership comprised four essential skills plus one

other factor that wasn't a skill, but was even more important. In other words, '4+1' didn't make five because it was like saying 4 apples plus 1 orange. So here. Zero or nothing is not a level or zone; it is the absence of a level or zone, for it is not there!

8   To be 0% motivated would almost certainly render the individual at a catatonic level of activity; in short, at this point we are not dealing with the typical workplace scenario but a chronic emotional condition in which the individual may well be in a state of serious depression or some other form of mental illness. Clearly, how we deal with this goes beyond the scope of this book, except in saying that maintaining high levels of motivation provides a very powerful antidote to this ever occurring in the first place. Dr Raj Persaud put it this way, 'A breakdown in motivation not only becomes self-fulfilling, but can also lead to severe psychological problems, if it leads to hopelessness and the feeling that things are not going to get better in the future', *Staying Sane* (Bantam Books, 1998).

9   One lesser known fact about the Motivational Maps is that they do not actually register motivation levels below 10%, and this is one reason why.

10 I am alluding here to the well-known FAB formula of selling, which talks of the Features, Advantages and Benefits of a product or service. See https://bit.ly/32QZWry.

11 It is true that at very senior levels in large organisations, public and private, lack of performance can go on for a very long time before it is uncovered; but uncovered it usually is as the cases, for examples, of Marconi and the Royal Bank of Scotland in the UK demonstrated, and the case of Enron showed in the USA. For a really detailed and convincing account of this phenomenon, see David Bowles and Cary Cooper, *The High Engagement Work Culture* (Palgrave Macmillan, 2012). Citing Phil Ebersole in Chapter 3, 'What he concluded from his research is that there was no relation – not even a negative relation – between what CEOs and other corporate executives got, and the performance of their companies … it was all random, he said'. This is perhaps the biggest corporate scandal of the twenty-first century: no performance and huge pay awards! However, the corruption within the system mustn't allow us to stop seeing that performance and reward are like hand and glove; they go together, and when they are uncoupled, the hand will eventually catch a fatal chill – if one may extend the metaphor.

12 And to accentuate this point: imagine that one had studied French at school 10 years ago and acquired a certificate in the subject. Once one had dropped studying it, one had not in 10 years gone back to it. However, one might get by, if one were in France, with the smattering of the language one had acquired; so one's performance in 'French' might be termed 'poor'. But if one had never studied French at all in one's life, then there would be no performance at all; this is what we mean when we say this is not a level at all.

13 I first encountered a version of this idea at a Tony Robbins' presentation in Wembley some 20 years or so ago, and was amazed at how insightful it was; I am almost equally amazed now in that I struggle to find any academic text that refers to this phenomenon, or any consultancy that seems to advocate its principles or insights into the condition of rewarding people in the work place.

14 Though even this assertion must be treated with caution. Lou Adler, a leading expert on recruitment, claimed that the average recruitment process produced a 50–50 chance of selecting the right candidate for the job. In other words, tossing a coin would be as likely to produce a good result! Lou Adler, *Hire with your Head: A Rational Way to make a Gut Reaction* (Wiley, 1998).

15 And sadly, average can often be construed as 'run-of-the-mill' or even 'medi-ocre'. Certainly, it is not a level of performance that draws much attention to itself; it does not 'stand out'.

16 'In 2010, the CIPD released a statistic that should concern any business leader: only 8% of people are "actively engaged" at work. In 2009, Kenexa ranked UK engagement levels at 9th among the 12 largest economies. Broadly speaking, 20 million British workers are not engaged, and therefore not reaching their potential' – Russell Beck, Impellam Group, Whitepaper, *Employee Engage-ment: Why it Matters, and How to Fix It* (2017).

17 This 'contractual arrangement' is on the one hand the specific job description which is generated from the contract of employment; but on the other hand it is also more than that. The term 'psychological contract' was according to J. Hiltrop, 'The changing psychological contract', *European Management Jour-nal*, Vol 13, No. 3, 1995, first coined by Chris Argyris in the 1970s, but which came into prominence in the 1990s through the work of Hiltrop and others. One useful comment on its relevance is: 'Now employees are expected to give more in terms of time, effort, skills, and flexibility, whereas they receive less in terms of career opportunities, lifetime employment, job security, and so on. Violation of the psychological contract is likely to produce burnout because it erodes the notion of reciprocity, which is crucial in maintaining well-being'. C. Maslach, W. Schaufeli and M. Leiter, 'Job burnout', *Annual Review Psychology* (52), 2001, p. 409. Psychological contracts are essentially a relationship between an employer and an employee where there are unwritten mutual expectations for each side. When these are not met, the employees engage in one of more of five categories of responses to the violations of psychological contract: they voice their views and attempt to repair the damage (healthy response); or less health-ily, they go silent, or retreat from their commitment and involvement; or, they become destructive or exit the organisation. *The Employee-Organization Rela-tionship: Applications for the 21st Century* (Applied Psychology Series), edited L. Shore et al. (Routledge, 2012).

18 Keep in mind, however, as Daniel Pink commented: 'We find that financial in-centives ... can result in a negative impact on overall performance' –*Drive: The Surprising Truth About What Motivates Us* (Canongate, 2010).

19 David Kolb et. al., *Organisational Psychology: A Book of Readings* (Prentice Hall, 1991).

20 No performance (0) of course begets no reward as nothing begets nothing, but it does not break the pattern because, as we have said, it is not really a level.

21 And for the avoidance of doubt, this lion or top dog may be in human terms female as well as male.

22 For more on the 'winning edge' see Dr Dennis Waitley, *The Winner's Edge: The Critical Attitude of Success*, reissue edition (Berkley Publishing Group, 1994).

23 As I write this, Lewis Hamilton has just won his sixth Formula 1 World Cham-pion title. It is instructive to look at the top seven F1 drivers in the world to see how this pans out, given that winning is down to tiny margins of performance. These are the highest-paid F1 drivers for the 2019 Season: #1 Lewis Hamilton (Mercedes) — $57M, #2 Sebastian Vettel (Ferrari) — $39.7M, #3 Daniel Ric-ciardo (Renault) — $34.5M, #4 Max Verstappen (Red Bull) — $13M, #5 Valtteri Bottas (Mercedes) — $8.5M, #6 Kimi Raikkonen (Alfa Romeo) — $4.5M, #7 Nico Hulkenberg (Renault) — $4.5M. The number 1 is earning nearly 70% more than the number 2, and once we consider the fourth fastest, their income is less than a quarter. But money is only part of it: as, say, Tiger Woods in golf in a recent generation, or Roger Federer in tennis, so Lewis Hamilton has become

a brand, a name, a reputation which fearsomely towers above all others in their specific domains. They get 'all' the praise, admiration and publicity relative to their competitors. Note that these are individuals, but the same applies to teams: football, basketball, rugby etc. The top teams receive a disproportionate share of the winnings or rewards.

24 The Pareto Principle would indicate that only 20% of people are high performers, meaning approaching excellence and going beyond. 20% of 20% gives us 4% of people likely to be truly outstanding, or even 20% of 20% of 20%, which is 0.8% or less than one person in a 100 may be truly outstanding!! A slightly depressing statistic. For more on this see *Mapping Motivation for Coaching*, ibid., Chapter 3, which also provides several sources for ideas on the Pareto Principle.

25 Donald G. Krause commented correctly, 'real distinction can only be earned by passing a true test of performance', *The Way of the Leader* (Nicholas Brealey, 1997). The word distinction implies outstanding performance, for it too suggests standing out.

26 The full quotation is from Virgil's *Aeneid*, Book 5, line 231 and part of it, 'Possunt, quia posse videntur' can be translated as 'They can because they think they can', which is similar to the more familiar quotation from Henry Ford: 'Whether you think you can, or you think you can't – you're right'. What these quotations establish is the importance of belief and how expectations, which are beliefs about the future, affect results, and if positive, then affect them positively.

27 See *Mapping Motivation*, ibid., and also *Mapping Motivation for Engagement*, ibid. for much more on this topic.

28 Even if pay were the only issue, the only motivator, as it were, it would still fail. Research by Michael Armstrong and Duncan Brown, *Strategic Reward* (Kogan Page India Private Limited, 2010) concludes there is no universally successful Performance Related Pay (PRP), no 'best practice, only best fit'. PRP's success is highly situational-specific. The implication of this is that leaders have to re-think what they are doing and offering their staff and their teams; there is no off-the-shelf solution.

29 See Duncan Brown, Institute for Employment Studies Paper, February 2018: https://bit.ly/2A5rcJB; and also Brown, D., West, M., 'Rewarding service? Using reward policies to deliver your customer service strategy', *WorldatWork*, Vol. 14, No. 4, (2005).

30 Duncan Brown, 'Fairness, flexibility and affordability: What are the lessons from recent pay and reward approaches and trends in the UK?' Institute for Employment Studies Paper, February 2018.

31 'Since the 2008 financial crisis, the UK's productivity has barely budged … . So perhaps the productivity puzzle is explained by lack of motivation. People are working longer and longer hours, in jobs that are increasingly insecure, for organisations focused solely on the bottom line. Is it any surprise that many workers feel demotivated?' – Jeremy Renwick, capx.co, *MoneyWeek*, 8/3/2019.

32 The expression is biblical: the labourer is worthy of his hire, suggesting that someone should be properly recompensed for their effort. It comes from Luke 10:7.

33 We might keep in mind Professor John Kay's harsh observation: 'There are people for whom money is an overwhelmingly dominant motivator, and who are primarily self-interested and opportunistic, but they are defective as human beings, and generally not suitable for employment in senior positions in complex organisations'. *MoneyWeek*, 1/2/2019.

34 Duncan Brown, ibid., 'The most commonly offered benefits' choices are: vaca-
    tion days; private medical cover; dental insurance; and health screening (Aon,
    2016). Financial education (26%), financial advice (20%), and "wellness" bene-
    fits are the fastest growing areas. Communications and costs are the main is-
    sues reported by employers, with UK employees at least initially appearing less
    well educated in determining their own rewards packages than is normal in the
    United States. Hence the majority of UK employers are planning to increase
    their communications over the next year. Total rewards statements are generally
    provided alongside flexible rewards and the research on their use is generally
    positive'.

Chapter 3

Getting to The Remit

Customer Focus for top performing teams

We saw in Chapter 1 that there were four primary team characteristics (see Figure 3.1) considered essential if the team were to be high performing. What we now need to do is to consider how to develop those four characteristics in an intelligent and sustainable way; furthermore, to see how motivation plays its part in all this, and how motivation can be deployed more effectively. Keep in mind two things: one, whatever the characteristics are, without motivation the team is dead in the water; and, two, as McKinsey observed[1] in their research, 'rewiring a company ... often [takes] 2 to 4 years'. In other words, there are no quick fixes; but that said, we can work towards immediate wins that take us towards the longer term goal we seek.

What, then, is the remit or mission of a team, and how do we strengthen and improve it? Also, what is the link with motivation? The remit is: what

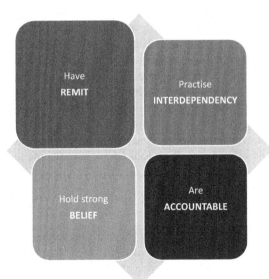

Figure 3.1 Have Remit

are we doing, when, where and for how long? And, for whom? Primarily, though, it appears as – what are we doing? This is not as easy to establish as it sounds. And note too that *when we do it* and *for how long* imply that simply having a job and turning up for work is not getting on with the remit; the remit is going to change over time, and so what we do will change with it. Herein is one motivational application: what we do feeds our motivators (or not) but if we have to change what we do, then will we still be motivated? Does the new remit float our boat in the way the previous one did? And aside from how we feel, how would a manager know if the remit was motivational or not?

The changes in the remit come about through various factors: organisational growth, innovations of products, services and systems, marketing developments, legislative changes, and most importantly from adopting a customer-centric approach to activities. Customers inevitably want changes/improvements, and organisations need to respond to that if they are to thrive. Indeed, in some sense the situations are far worse than customers simply wanting changes or improvements: customers even when the service or product is really good may want to swap suppliers merely because they are bored by the provision that they have and think that a new provider might just provide something extra that they feel is missing in the existing provision. Perhaps the only way to guarantee – and can we guarantee? – retention of a customer/client is by achieving the very highest levels of customer service,[2] but what are they?

Since we are dealing with top performing teams in this book, it would be good to take a look at a model of customer performance at this point so that we are clear about what we are trying to do. After all, to be 'top performing' there must be a relationship to some goal that we are attempting to realise. For many organisations such a goal would be entirely financial: a top performing team would be the team that generates the most revenue, or profit, or which cuts costs most effectively. Such a view would be severely limited, because it would a) make increasing earnings the purpose of an organisation, rather than an outcome resulting from a higher purpose, and b) it would contradict the whole philosophy of Motivational Mapping, since it would imply that everyone is motivated by money or the Builder motivators, which is palpably false. Indeed, we looked at this at some length at the end of Chapter 2.

Activity 3.1

What, then, are the levels of customer service that we need to consider, and which top performing teams need to aim for? How many levels of customer service are there, and how would you characterise them? A clue might be that the answer may not surprise you, given what we have covered about performance so far!

There are, unsurprisingly, four levels of customer service, as there are four levels of performance[3] and four levels of motivation; plus, of course, one, where one equals zero. In other words, where there is no customer service at all. So just as we have observed that it is possible to have no performance at all, and this means invariably that one is out of a job or a task or commission because one is doing nothing or something chaotically irrelevant, so too it is possible to encounter a business or organisation where the level of customer service is so lamentably absent that they cannot survive long, even given a unique product that people want. Perhaps the best example of zero customer service is the sort of business that one can frequently (though not always) experience in a local market or bazaar: often products are arranged or scattered in a not particularly useful or helpful way, the attendant simply wants to take money for the product and there is little interaction or warmth, and there is certainly no follow-up or warranty.

But a top performing team is going to be critically aware of the four levels of customer service as an essential outcome of their performance and a key measure of it. The four levels of customer service match the four levels of performance.

A poor level of service is where one gets what you pay for and nothing more. One enters a cafeteria, queues, helps oneself to what is there, and gets to pay at the end. Then one collects one's own knives and forks to find an available table to sit at. When finished, one puts the empty plates and cups on a tray, and puts the tray where it can be collected for washing-up. Simple, basic, and nobody gets excited by this level of service or returns because of it; we only use it because it might be very cheap or it might be the only convenient place around. Ultimately, businesses like this quickly go out of business.

The good level of service, by way of contrast, is more like the restaurant where you get seated by a waiter or waitress; you may be able to book in advance; the menu is much wider; the quality of food is better; and there is service. This is good but that is all; in one sense it is only fulfilling the plain

Performance Directed to Customer Service	Descriptors	Motivation
4	Outstanding	Optimal
3	Excellent	Boost
2	Good	Risk
1	Poor	Action
0		

Figure 3.2 The four levels of customer service

expectations we have in going to a restaurant at all. The poor service was purely basic; the good service is more functional, but it certainly has no frills or extras.

However, when we get to excellent service things change yet again. Here the customer has been seriously thought about: not just – if we take the restaurant analogy – in the sense that they want to eat something because they are hungry, but in the sense of what they want as part of being human: they want exceptional experiences, they want respect and civility, they want sensory delights beyond merely food and drink, though including that too. So in the excellent restaurant we find a very careful selection of foods and drinks, we find staff who have been well trained and who interact positively with customers, we find a special décor, a particular ambience, perhaps music, and a selection of items (including the cutlery, plates, tablecloth, seating etc.) which have also chosen to enhance the experience. But especially we find that sense of being attended to personally.

Finally, at the level of outstanding service we find ourselves astonished or amazed by the level of product and service. This is where the restaurant goes the extra mile, where the smallest of details can become significant in terms of the whole experience: for example, the waiter remembers one's name and where one likes to sit, and perhaps other facts of one's life which they enquire about – 'How is your son in his new job?'. They probably know your birthday and make a fuss when you go in. It's where there are complimentary ('free'!) benefits and discounts; and it's also where if one's coat, hat, wallet has been accidentally mislaid, you can be sure that they will contact you and even offer to return it to you, either physically or by post. And it's where change is endemic: they are constantly thinking of new ways to improve the service, update the menu and provide stimulation and interest, for they know that 'sameness' ultimately becomes boring even when it is excellent.

Activity 3.2

Consider who your customers or clients are.[4] How would you rate your own personal customer service level: is it non-existent, poor, good, excellent or outstanding? And then consider the team you may be a part of, or a team that works closely nearby within your organisation, or a team that you have observed in action. How would you rate them? Given the service descriptors we have depicted, what reasons would you give for your ranking?

If we look at Figure 3.2 we see that motivation and customer service performance levels both have four levels (plus the zero of no motivation and no service). As we know from earlier work,[5] whilst there may not be an immediate correlation between these two dimensions, in the long run they are certainly going to correlate. How could outstanding levels of customer service be performed without there being a corresponding uptick in energy, in motivation? Clearly, one presupposes the other.

Figure 3.3 Ritz-Carlton Credo or remit or mission[6]

A great example – sticking with the 'restaurant' services sector – of outstanding service is contained in the Ritz-Carlton Credo. The word 'Credo' means 'I believe' – we are reaching the point of the remit or the mission that we talked of earlier; the remit that was essential for a top performing team.

The above remit or mission statement in Figure 3.3 is really quite remarkable in several ways. If we take the first sentence, perhaps the most remarkable word is 'genuine': can hotel employees genuinely care for their customers? Indeed, imagine that aspiration being transposed to your organisation – can we genuinely care for our customers and clients? What does it take to be *genuine*?

The second sentence is also pretty amazing and aspirational. Here the key word is 'pledge'; that's a very strong word. Not 'try' or 'attempt' to provide, but pledge to do it, as if it were an oath; like knights of old we are pledged together to achieve the Holy Grail of complete customer satisfaction![7] Imagine your teams 'pledged' to achieve the mission – do you think that the pledge alone might have an impact on the performance?

Finally, the third sentence contains the most astonishing clause of all, absolutely astonishing.

Activity 3.3

Which part of that third sentence, which clause, is really and truly astonishing? And since the sentence isn't that long, why is this clause astonishing? What are its true implications?

The clause that deserves our attention is 'fulfils even the *unexpressed wishes* and needs of our guests'. That, if understood in its entirety, is little short of staggering as an aspiration. Why? Because it is something that can only come about as an act of 'love'! We barely – most of the time – can understand what our friends, children and partners want when they directly express their desires to us; to understand what somebody wants but who hasn't expressed it overtly requires extremely high levels of intuition, empathy and experience, since it can scarcely come naturally. It is in other words virtually the highest level of service that one can contemplate: staff – the teams at Ritz-Carlton – are being asked to anticipate customer needs in a way that is intimate, personal and effective; this is a million miles away from the bazaar or street market of zero customer service that we mentioned earlier.

And one person cannot do it; it has to be a team effort to function in this way, or else individuals would be overwhelmed with the pressure and simply burn out. That is why, when one drills down in the specifics of what Ritz-Carlton demands of its employees we find 'basics' like: 'Create a positive work environment. Practise team work and lateral service'. Practise teamwork – in order to do what? To achieve the remit. And together – as in T.E.A.M[8] – each achieves more by virtue of the support, encouragement modelling of good behaviours that top performing teams inevitably produce.

Before coming specifically to the building of teams, we might want to reflect on the practicalities of these abstractions. When we talk of *genuineness*, or *pledges* or *unexpressed wishes*, this can seem somewhat idealistic and remote from everyday life, especially perhaps in a hotel where working is by its very nature extremely practical. Indeed, Ritz-Carlton suggests as much when it refers to its staff creating what it calls 'The Ritz-Carlton Mystique'! Mystique – another airy-fairy word. But again we see that having ideals, values and/or a remit is not airy-fairy at all but exceedingly practical.

These three steps in Figure 3.4 are part of a much wider package of practical things to do to realise the remit. But see how simple they are: 'a warm and sincere greeting'. But as with the word 'genuine', it takes real practice to get to 'sincere'. However, if we don't start, we will never get there.

And this is not rocket science really. To take another example: the well-known and highly successful UK high street retailer Richer Sounds has ten things they expect their top performing teams to do. Figure 3.5 provides an abbreviated version of them.

Notice the centrality of the greeting in both Figure 3.4 and 3.5. This makes total sense: we have one chance to make a good first impression, and to be outstanding at customer service is to take it.

Let's take a look, then, at what we call The Outstanding Index. Here in Figure 3.6 is an abridged form of it. The list of activities that one may need to be 'outstanding' at in any given sector may be considerable. In the case,

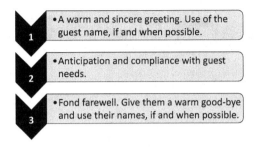

1   • A warm and sincere greeting. Use of the guest name, if and when possible.

2   • Anticipation and compliance with guest needs.

3   • Fond farewell. Give them a warm good-bye and use their names, if and when possible.

Figure 3.4 The Ritz-Carlton three steps of service

1	Get the greeting right.
2	Don't be pushy.
3	Browsers are welcome.
4	If the item wanted is not in stock, suggest where else they can find it.
5	Use the customer's name. And SMILE.
6	Acknowledge customers who are queuing & apologise for keeping them waiting.
7	The last minute is very important. Do everything to ensure a good impression.
8	Under promise and over deliver.
9	Encourage complaints and... then learn from them.
10	Don't be discouraged when you get it wrong. Keep at it.

Figure 3.5 Ten pointers for The Richer Way

for example, of the Ritz-Carlton they list 20 Basics; other types of organisations may have more or less. But in our Outstanding Index we have reduced the key activities to what we consider the most important five. These five are more or less applicable to any organisation, anywhere, and failure in any of them is likely to be serious in terms of consequences.

In considering Activity 3.4 there should already be enough information in this chapter to be clear about what the various levels are for customer-oriented mission, standards of performance and attitude and motivation. Regarding behaviour, we can consider this as including how individuals,

Customer Care	Don't know – Thoughtless – Poor	Same as everyone else – Good	Better – Excellent	Amazing – Outstanding
1. Customer-oriented mission				
2. Standards of performance				
3. Attitude and motivation				
4. Behaviour				
5. Appearance				

Figure 3.6 The Outstanding Index

teams and the whole organisation behave, depending on the size of the organisation. Clearly, how individuals behave towards us impacts us most, as does how they appear. But going into any organisation, we immediately also start forming judgements based on appearances too. Now look at Activity 3.4.

Activity 3.4

Complete The Outstanding Index for your organisation or business. Rate yourself and your team as honestly as you can. Then, when you have done this, invite other team members (in the first place) or other colleagues to do the same. Compare your results. Investigate where there are widely differing scores. How does the team you are in address the issues that arise from this analysis? Make a list of the things that need to be done, when and by whom. Remember, the key thing for a top performing team to do is to deliver 'outstanding' service.[9] Ensure that you are very clear on that.

Activity 3.5

Imagine now that Figure 3.6 has some extra scoring information: Poor is 1 point, Good is 2, Excellent is 3, and Outstanding is 4. Give yourself points for how you rate your Outstanding Index. The maximum score is 20 if you had given yourself 4 points (Outstanding) for each of the five areas of customer care. Convert this to a percentage by multiplying by 5. And again we have four quadrants of performance: 80% and above is outstanding, 60–79% is excellent, 35–59% is good, and below 35% is poor. As with motivational quadrants, below 35% means immediate and remedial Action, 35–59%

means one is in the Risk Zone (the Risk here being the business will fail!), 60–79% means you are in the Boost Zone (so that with a little more effort you could achieve Outstanding service) and finally 80% and above you are likely to be providing Outstanding service. The challenge of 80% and above is to sustain it for the long term.

We have, spent some time considering the importance of the customer in determining our remit or mission. So let us now look at the word remit itself and use this as our central concept for working alongside the Motivational Map. The word remit, used as a noun – the remit – basically means the task or area of activity officially assigned to an individual, team or organisation; it also has the connotation of being the matter submitted for consideration.[10] Tasks or activities are what we do, and in this way we can think of the remit as being the same as the mission. But in having a remit – if we consider this the matter for 'consideration' – there are three distinct areas to focus on; what we do is one of them, the customer and their expectations is another; but finally, if we are going to have a top performing team (or individual or organisation) then the values we insist on are crucial. Hence, The Remit for a top performing team comprises three elements, as shown in Figure 3.7.

In studying this we see three elements of The Remit and we need to realise that they are all interconnected in a profound way, and that motivation is at the heart of all three elements as we shall show. But firstly we must point out that this is what we think a remit really is; not just a task, without any further consideration, but something far more intrinsic, deeper, aligned to

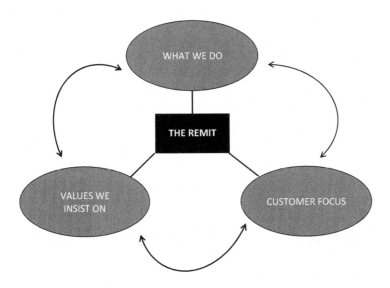

Figure 3.7 Three elements of The Remit

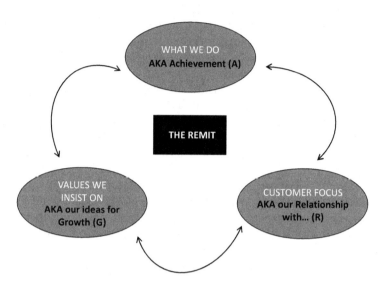

Figure 3.8 RAG and the three elements of The Remit

human nature and desires, and ultimately highly productive. The point of a top performing team is to be productive, and superior productivity leads to improved profits or organisational results. We cannot cover every aspect of The Remit in a book this size, but what we can cover are the motivational aspects of it, and show how motivation is central.

A cursory moment's thought – and viewing Figure 3.8 – will show that each of the three elements has a dominant link to one of the three motivational groupings expressed as R–A–G: Relationship–Achievement–Growth. In starting this chapter, we examined the Customer Focus (or Service if you will) as a primary starting point. But what exactly is a customer focus? If we review what we said about the Ritz-Carlton approach we realise that the essence of a customer (or client or patient) approach is relationship driven; for we seek to understand the customer in such a way that if we can truly understand them, then this will lead almost to a form of 'love'. This applies whether we are dealing with the obvious case of hotel service and its one-to-one interactions, or the less obvious case where we manufacture 100 million bottles of shampoo for world-wide distribution: even in the latter case, the smart organisation is going to think very carefully about the customers (the countries, the languages, the customs and values, the colours even, and so on) if they are going to have the remotest chance of shifting all those bottles! Branding itself is about first forming a relationship in the very mind of the customer. It is inescapable, therefore, that relationship building is at the heart of the customer focus.

This, we remember, is at the base of the Maslow Hierarchy of Needs,[11] and accords with the Relationship type motivators in Motivational Maps: the Defender, Friend and Star type motivators relate very strongly, though not exclusively, with Customer Focus for The Remit.

Activity 3.6

How, then, do you think this information might be useful in the construction of a top performing team?

Keep in mind, both that teams are not driven solely by one motivator, but usually the top three have an influence on their preoccupations; secondly, that the R motivators are not exclusively the motivators of Customer Focus. For example, the Expert or the Searcher may well be interested in and concentrated on Customer Focus. But here's the difference that we really need to keep centrally in mind: for the Expert, Customer Focus or Care is a matter of the mind (that is, Thinking), of expertise itself, of working out exactly how we are going to serve the customer. What we call the Head.[12] And for the Searcher the Customer Focus is a matter of making that difference that they strive to do from, as it were, their Body or Gut; it's the right and direct thing to do and it follows from Knowing what to do, and so they do it. What is different about the Defender and Friend motivators principally is that the desire to serve the customer comes from the Heart, and so from Feeling, and it is that Feeling state that gives it an edge.

The edge derives from the fact that the Heart sees things differently from the Head or the Body; indeed, it might be better to say that it *feels* things differently from them, and whilst feelings can sometimes mislead and provide distortions to perceptions of reality, in this case we want to know what our customers 'feel'. We want to be able to empathise with their situation so that our product or service can really solve their problem, issue or need. This is where the Heart motivators are most relevant. Sure, the Expert may provide superior thinking power and analysis of the situation, but this can often be at the expense of what we might call the human dimension or factor; and we are very familiar with this problem in management itself.

If we look at Figure 3.9 and consider what we know about motivational distribution from over 70,000 maps that have been completed, then we understand that asking the Defenders and Friend motivator types[13] about how to serve the customer more effectively is exactly what happens whenever an organisation asks its employees and teams to contribute to solving customer issues and improving the service or product. For, although all motivators can be found in all individuals at all levels within an organisation, the reality is that the hierarchy, mirroring Maslow's, attracts certain types, and for obvious motivational reasons.

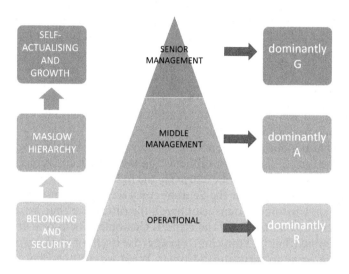

Figure 3.9 Motivational distribution according to RAG

The Defender, for example, is risk averse: generally speaking, the higher one goes in an organisation, the riskier one's position is.[14] Conversely, the Creator who wishes to innovate can usually only do so when at a certain and higher point in the organisational structure. Of course, these ideas are not immutable, and advanced and engaged organisations turn these ideas on their head, but as a general principle, we see more Defenders and Friends at the lower reaches of the organisational hierarchy.

And we know that it is precisely at that end of the pyramid that the best ideas for solving and improving the customer experience are to be found, because they are working closest with the customers![15] If we then add into the mix the idea of the Defender and Friend being precisely these kind of people,[16] then we have a methodology for improving the customer experience, service or product. It is good that senior management seeks to involve and engage operational staff in the innovation necessary to improve services and products for the customer, but the extra edge and what might be the way forward is in actively seeking out what the operational staff who are specifically Defender- and Friend-motivated (and to a lesser extent Star-motivated) actually 'think' or in fact *feel*.

This is a breakthrough perception (even though it may take a longer time to deliver) for senior management; for if we think about it, we have a double benefit. On the one hand, we have operational staff who work with the delivery of the service or product on a daily basis and, on the other, we have those staff who are most aligned with what the customer wants emotionally. The Defender seeks to get things right, to be efficient, and to drive value for money; the Friend genuinely wants to help the customer, sees the customer as the raison d'être of the teamwork they are practising, and indeed may see them as belonging to, or be an extension of, their team. Thus, although the Defender and Friend motivator-types may not be the most knowledgeable or innovative, they really want to deliver on The Remit. As we know, where there is that kind of attitude, there is usually a corresponding kind of result.

But as I said, this may take time, for we also know that in terms of speed, the Relationship motivators tend to be slow, since they are risk averse. It is clearly a balancing act or judgement call rather akin to the tortoise and the hare fable. Slow and steady can sometimes outperform the fast and impatient! However, it is important to recognise just how useful the Defender and Friend motivator types can be in team work and in creating improved solutions for the customer.

What might this mean in practice? Let's take a situation in which we have a Motivational Map of a top performing team, but in which the Friend and Defender motivators are low.

Here is a map of a highly successful team working in the high-tech sector (Figure 3.10). The first sign that they are a top performing team is simply their motivational score: 79%, which is almost in the Optimal Zone, and which for eight people is a very strong result. We note that the score probably would be in the Zone but for one member at 59%. As a leader of the team we would want to look closely at that particular map and consider what some of the issues might be.[17] However, if we consider the Defender and Friend motivators, what might we find?

Top Motivator
Second Motivator
Third Motivator
Lowest Motivator

Team Motivation Score: 79%

Change Index Score: 59

RAG: 31-32-37

Name	Searcher	Builder	Spirit	Creator	Star	Expert	Defender	Director	Friend	Motivation Audit			
										%	1	2	3
JON	26	22	24	17	23	16	23	19	10	80%	9	6	8
ANDY	17	28	21	20	22	20	22	17	13	84%	9	7	9
DON	19	19	18	19	21	22	24	13	25	80%	9	6	8
GEOFF	20	21	20	19	22	19	24	15	20	59%	6	6	5
ANT	22	26	21	18	16	27	15	21	14	75%	8	6	9
CATHY	32	13	21	23	17	28	17	10	19	81%	8	8	9
ANDREW	27	23	23	14	22	10	21	19	21	76%	8	7	7
GILL	30	26	28	34	19	15	9	14	5	97%	10	10	7
Total	193	178	176	164	162	157	155	128	127	79%			

Figure 3.10 Team data table with Friend lowest

Activity 3.7

How might the team strengthen its customer focus by considering the Defender and the Friend motivators? What issues are there to consider here?

The first thing to mention is what the top three motivators suggest to us in terms of customer service. That Searcher is the top motivator, and that no-one in the team has it lowest or has it below 10/40 (the lowest is 17), indicates a team which wants to make a difference for the customer or client; so far, so good. They are also competitive (Builder), which can also be good in terms of driving up standards, although a potential downside might be a commercial orientation that might exploit the customer and perhaps tip the balance from great value to over-pricing. Thirdly, the Spirit motivator is relatively high across all the members, and with Director so low, suggests that the team is more a group of high powered individuals who like to perform – that is specifically, to make a difference to their particular customers – rather than act in a co-ordinated team way. This is reinforced, of course, by the fact that Friend is the lowest motivator of all. People in this team are not coming to work to belong or for social reasons, which means they are likely to be without a strong feeling that they need to support each other.

With these preliminary observations out of the way, then, how can the Friend and Defender motivators help the customer get a better deal – improve the service or product?

Typically, we might ask the team in a session or on some away-day designed around this purpose (to improve the customer experience) just this question: how do we improve our offering? And there will be many good answers to it: the two Creators, especially, will have innovative ideas to put forward, and in the case of Gill, a spike[18] of 34/40, there will be a real passion to put forward new ideas. Equally, perhaps, we have three members motivated by expertise, and two of them (Ant and Cathy, 27/40, 28/40) with relatively high scores; so they will wish to contribute to the HOW of what we do next. And, of course, any well-informed member of the team may have good ideas.

But I would suggest here that the leader of the team (Jon) needs to speak privately with Don and ask for Don's advice. We see that Don is seriously the outsider of the team – sharing none of the top three motivators of the whole team in his own profile – but yet is still highly motivated at 80%, and so almost certainly functioning at a high level. The fact of asking for Don's advice or help is itself a very 'Friend' way of approaching a Friend-motivated type of person. And note that Don has Friend as his number one motivator, alongside Defender as his second. Clearly, Don is a Relationship-driven type of person; he is driven by his Heart, or feeling. Finally, the added benefit of asking him is that he has Expert as his third motivator, so he is likely to have an analytic bent too. Perfect!

Activity 3.8

Imagine that you are Jon, Don's boss, and you want to ask Don about improving Customer Service, what three questions might you ask him? Be clear about how you would frame them.

Three good questions that might well get the best out of someone like Don might be:

Set-up or permission question:

1. Don, I hope you don't mind, but I wanted to talk to you personally for your help because I know from what I've seen of your work, and also from your Motivational Map profile, that you really care about our customers perhaps in a way that others don't quite get. Are you happy to help me here?

Actual question:

2. I'm concerned that we are not doing all we could for our customers, and that we could add a lot more value in our offerings to them. What do you think we could do to be better in this (specific) area?

Follow-up question:

3. That's some great ideas. How do you think we can sell this to the rest of the team? And how can we implement this to your customers afterwards? Is there a time frame you have in mind?

What we are doing here is using the Motivational Maps within a team framework to identify potential individual strengths to improve a core aspect of The Remit, specifically, the customer experience.

Activity 3.9

As it happens, there is only one team member with Friend in their top three profile. But there are four people with Defender. Geoff has the joint highest score (with Don) at 24/40. However, would we ask Geoff in the same way we have Don? What do you think, and give reasons or a reason for your answer? And if not Geoff, who might be asked?

Actually, we probably would not ask Geoff (unless we had some reason that is not apparent in the Map alone). The central reason we would not ask him is because unlike Don his motivational score is only 59%: he is in the Risk Zone and is clearly not happy with his current situation. Interestingly, he scores his second and third motivators, Star and Builder, as only 6/10 and 5/10 respectively, so he is unhappy with the pay and his personal recognition. It suggests he is not really fitting in; asking him for help might boost his Star motivation – and this is a judgement call that Jon would have to make – but it is probably unlikely. At a certain point a low motivational score means that one spends more time thinking about one's own situation than one does how customers are experiencing the service, and so the advice is not likely to be insightful.

If we had to choose one extra person, then it would probably be Andy, who has a Defender and Star combination. This means that two of this three top motivators are Relationship driven and so like Don, though not to the same extent, he will have a more feeling-based as well as systematic view of what might work for the customer. And, unlike Geoff, Andy is 84% motivated, suggesting a high performer.

Interestingly, of course, the other team member who has Defender in their top three is Jon himself, the leader, and asking himself is not going to be useful here! But note, how Jon asking Andy is particularly helpful in that Jon's own top three motivators are dominantly Growth, at the other end of the spectrum from Andy. In short, we are getting motivational diversity here – the good leader is going to be someone who realises that their own motivational perspectives need challenging and, for Jon, Andy (keeping in mind that Don is even more so) could provide that different way of looking at issues.

In this chapter we have covered what we consider The Remit for top performing teams to be and provided some detailed analysis of the Relationship component which relates to a Customer Focus. Let's also not forget what we said in Chapter 2 about Reward Strategies: given how we have positioned the Friend motivator in this study, why not check out the Team Friend Motivators in the Resources Section to see if anything there might work here?

Our next chapter will look at the second component of The Remit – What We Do – and investigate its motivational elements.

Notes

1 Ewan Duncan, 'In order to rewire a company to become a customer experience leader for most companies this will be a two-to-three-to-four-year journey' – The CEO Guide to Customer Experience, March 2016, https://bit.ly/2XBa8Di
2 Abraham Lincoln observed that 'The only security you can ever have is the ability to do your job uncommonly well' – and what is true for the individual, applies equally to the team. Cited in *Victory! Applying the Proven Principles of Military Strategy to Achieve Greater Success in Your Business & Personal Life*, Brian Tracy (TarcherPerigree, Penguin Random House, 2017). Also note, 'Customer service has become so important today that every successful business is in the service business' – Leonard Goodstein, *Applied Strategic Thinking* (McGraw-Hill, 1993).
3 These four levels are actually four plus one, where one equals zero; in other words, no performance or motivation or service at all. It doesn't count as a level since it is a complete absence or negation. But there are four levels because the

Pareto Principle is based on an 80/20 ratio, or 4 to 1, and this also seems to intuitively fit our understanding of performance. For more on the Pareto Principle and Mapping Motivation, see *Mapping Motivation*, James Sale (Routledge, 2016) and especially *Mapping Motivation for Coaching*, James Sale and Bevis Moynan (Routledge, 2018), Chapter 3.

4   Actually, if you work for an organisation you will doubtless believe your customer/client is whoever your boss says it is; but the reality for all employees, especially cost centres, is that your real customer is your immediate boss (that is to say, internally directed), since without their support your own career and progress is likely to be severely handicapped. Furthermore, within most organisations some teams are outward facing, that is, directly to and for the customer, whereas others are inwardly directed: administration or HR for example. But whoever the customer is, the top performing team will be driven to supply outstanding levels of service.

5   See *Mapping Motivation*, ibid., Chapter 5.

6   As with all organisations mission statements are updated over time, and we have used one particular incarnation of their remit. For the latest go to: https://bit.ly/34vJfCg

7   It is worth reflecting for a moment on this mythological image of King Arthur's Knights of the Round Table, for it is a symbol for a top performing team. King Arthur may be the CEO, but remember the table is round, so that all are considered equal. Also, the knights are valued specifically for their own special skills and talents. True, Lancelot may be the bravest or strongest, but the stories of the others are equally important, and they all shine in their turn. Only treachery – that is, sabotage from within – ultimately defeats them; it is not an external enemy or competitor. If we think of the demise of most organisations which were once successful, we find that internal problems account for most of the collapses which occur.

8   T.E.A.M. is an acronym standing for Together Each Achieves More.

9   According to Gartner, 'With 89% of businesses soon to be expected to compete mainly on customer experience, organizations that take customer experience seriously will stand out from the noise and win loyal customers' – https://bit.ly/38b8HPy

10   *The Chambers Dictionary*, Tenth Edition, 2006.

11   See *Mapping Motivation*, ibid., Chapter 2.

12   For much more on RAG and the Heart, Head and Body connection, See *Mapping Motivation*, ibid., Chapter 3. Also, *Mapping Motivation for Coaching*, ibid., Chapter 4.

13   The Star motivator is also a Relationship motivator, but it has special properties that sometimes run counter to the Friend and Defender motivators. More aspects of the Star motivator are discussed in Chapters 6 and 7.

14   For the reason that the 'buck stops here'. Though in cartels and country clubs there will be exceptions to this general rule.

15   We have cited this research in the previous chapter, but it is worth repeating here: according to Sydney Yoshida, 'The Iceberg of Ignorance, Quality Improvement and TQM at Calsonic in Japan and Overseas' (1989), the top executives are only aware of 4% of the problems, the team managers of 9%, the team leaders of 74% and the staff of 100%! – https://bit.ly/2DNPae5

16   Not forgetting of course that individual's motivators change over time, and so one is not stereotyped. Indeed, the journey from being an operative to CEO of an organisation may well be accompanied by a radical shift in one's motivators.

17   Three obvious points for reflection might be: that Geoff only shares one of the top three motivators of the team; he feels underpaid for his contributions, since he scores his Builder only 5/10; and finally, although the spread of his scores is 9 (15–24), these two motivators are outriders, for the majority of his motivators are clustered around the 20 score – in other words, there is a distinct lack of differentiation in his motivators which may lead to indecision and indecisiveness.

18   A 'spike' is a score of 30 or above, and indicates a particularly intense desire for this motivator. An inverse spike (scores of 10 or below which signal the motivator is becoming more an aversion than desire) shows, as the name indicates, the reverse situation.

Chapter 4

Getting to The Remit
What We Do

We now pursue our investigation into The Remit. In Chapter 3 we examined the Relationship (the R of RAG) aspect of this and how top performing teams had to keep the customer in the forefront of their thinking if they were to continue as a top performing team. The word 'thinking' here, of course, we extended to mean 'feeling': in essence there were motivators that are specifically about 'feeling' and consulting team members who were driven by these motivators could make a massive difference to the outcomes for the customer as well as for the organisation.

The second strand of The Remit that needs to be consciously addressed by the top performing team is the 'What We Do' component. We linked this with what in Motivational Mapping we call the Achievement-type (the A of RAG) motivators that are very expressly connected to what organisations, and certainly businesses, see as their primary goal.

To be very clear about this, and provocative too, many businesses seem[1] oblivious to issues such as belonging (Friend), security (Defender), or recognition (Star) at the Relationship (R) end of motivation; and equally can be blasé or indifferent to innovation (Creator), autonomy (Spirit) or even making a difference for their customers (Searcher). But, is any organisation or business unmindful of power or control (Director), money or resources (Builder) or even expertise or skills (Expert)? One would struggle to think of one, except in the sense of some utopian project that very quickly went out of business!

The reality is that the Achievement motivators (Director, Builder, and Expert) define for most people what running an organisation is all about, and even non-profit organisations have to focus on where the finance comes from. Therefore, typically, making things happen in order to get 'achievement' in an organisation, we see what is in Figure 4.1.

Things 'happen', then, because management controls resources (money) and develops expertise, which leads to service or product creation, and customers pay more money for this and so the cycle continues. Of course, what

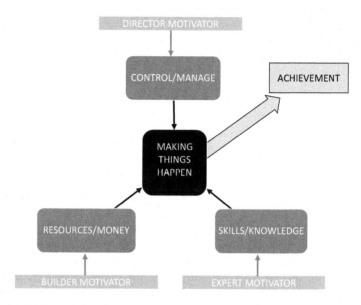

Figure 4.1 Making things happen in organisations

I have deliberately omitted from this illustration of making things happen, or 'achievement', is the people dimension: money[2] may not be a person, but management is made up of people, and the expertise also resides in people, even if machines and computers can sometimes provide expertise. Even in this situation somebody has to interpret or convey this information in some way. People are at the heart of organisations, yet sometimes you'd never guess so; it all seems to be brains or in certain cases muscle and sinew (where there is a large physical component to the work – for example, fruit-picking on a farm).

When things are not happening – when achievement is lacking – the typical tendency of organisations is to do more of what they do! They double-down on what they are doing. So management needs more management,[3] more money needs to be invested, and more training and/or expertise are needed. Of course, this may be perfectly correct. But there is a big motivational danger.

Activity 4.1

From a motivational point of view, what might be the dangers of an organisation responding to a crisis by imposing more management, or supplying more resources as made available by more money, or by developing greater expertise? Remember that any two or all three might simultaneously be supplied: more money might, for example, be spent on training for managers. Think about your answer purely from the point of view of the nine motivators.

Here we have a fascinating scenario that can easily become counterproductive from an organisational or business perspective. First, if management decides to tighten up – usually under the guise of improving – there is invariably an increase in the scope of the authority of the managers. The danger here is that the Director motivator becomes over-dominant and in particular begins to suppress its opposite motivator, the Spirit. In other words, there is increasing micro-management which is demotivating for the Spirit motivated, and these may include some of the managers themselves. Indeed, we have frequently observed, in the SME business market specifically, many Managing Directors combine the Director and Spirit motivator in their top three.

Similarly, the overuse of money, however it be deployed, can lead to the perception that all problems are solvable through financial means, and that only money counts when dealing with issues. This of course is dangerous motivationally for those who are Searcher motivated. And this is doubly dangerous because in our research the Searcher is by far and away the most common motivator in an individual's top three.[4] A wholly commercial approach to achievement, therefore, is likely to be demotivating for a large number of employees at all levels, and this includes (see Figure 3.9) top management.

Finally, and seemingly innocently, the over-commitment to developing expertise can also create problems. In particular, it can stifle innovation or the Creator motivator. Expert and Creator often go together as a pair in happy harmony: deep knowledge can lead to innovations and new ideas; but equally, expertise that is too process and systems driven can stifle innovation, and there becomes one right way of doing things which no-one ever challenges alternatives. This is particularly true when a strong Expert motivator is combined with a strong Defender motivator. In such situations, a risk-averse caution to new ideas tends to creep in, and knowledge can become fossilised.

In a way these dangers are aspects of what we called in another context hygiene factors.[5] The strong focus in one or some limited area, such as Achievement (A), can lead us to overlook the importance of other motivators that may be necessary to drive through success in the longer term. We cannot easily change individuals' motivators in the short-term, but the more self-aware we are of what the necessary motivators are in a given situation, or goal, the more likely we are to be able to create the right balance and emphasis in terms of the team motivational profile.

To illustrate this in some detail consider Figure 4.2.[6]

Rank order of over 5000 Maps in ten sectors	Builder	Creator	Defender	Director	Expert	Friend	Searcher	Spirit	Star
Accounting			2				1	3	L
Government Administration			3		2		1		L
Human Resources					3		1	2	L
Information Technology					2		1	3	L
Pharmaceuticals			3		2		1		L
Marketing and Advertising		3					1	2	L
Financial Services	3		2				1		L
Health Wellness and Fitness					2		1	3	L
Insurance			3		2		1		L
Construction			3		2		1		L
Rank Order	5	6	4	8	2	7	1	3	9
Rounded %	7.7	6.8	11.5	3.3	13	3.9	40.8	11.6	1.4

Figure 4.2 Rank order of over 5000 Maps in ten sectors

Activity 4.2

Figure 4.2 represents an analysis of over 5000 Motivational Maps carried out on ten sectors over a period of time. The sectors have been selected merely to exhibit variety; the Maps were done in various organisations across the whole organisation, and so employees at all levels were mapped, although the majority in this sample were at the middle and senior management levels. Specifically, here we are looking at the frequency with which a motivator was ranked first, or top, by an individual. So we see, for example, more than 40% of the mappers ranked Searcher as their number one motivator. Indeed, we see across the ten sectors that Searcher was by a considerable margin ranked first. Keeping in mind that the sample size (~5000 Maps) is relatively small and that we are not taking the roles or seniority of the staff who participated into account, what preliminary observations would you make on this table of results? List three points that you think might be important.

Given what we are talking about here – what we do and how this aligns or does not align with our motivators – a number of important issues arise.

First, as we have already discussed, though organisations can be preoccupied with Achievement-type motivators – Director, Builder and Expert – the reality seems to be that few organisations have people in them who actually want to manage (Director) and surprisingly who want to make money (Builder). From the sample we see that only 3.3% of individuals had Director as their number one motivator and it does not appear in the top three of any of the ten sectors. And, although the Builder motivator is doubly more common than Director at 7.7%, it still features only as third in the ranking and in just one of the ten sectors – Financial Services! Well, that makes sense, since you'd think Financial Services might employ people preoccupied with money; but, then again, presumably you'd think the same about cognate sectors such as Accounting and Insurance, but Builder does not feature in their top three. So it appears for all the hype, will-power and cultural norms around being in control – managing – and making money, at some deeper level employees – at all levels – largely want something else.[7]

Second, the dominance and frequency of the Searcher motivator needs careful consideration and explanation.[8] What is particularly significant about this phenomenon, which we have noticed in other samples that we have taken, is that Searcher is at the top of the motivational pyramid (and Maslow's Hierarchy) and is the motivator pre-eminently concerned with making a difference or 'WHY'? In other words, it is the motivator of purpose. As Simon Sinek[9] expressed it, 'WHAT companies do are external factors, but WHY they do it is something deeper'. And he goes on to say, 'In business, like a bad date, many companies work so hard to prove their value without saying WHY they exist in the first place'. So we come to the fundamental position of saying that what we do has to be underpinned by a purpose, or a WHY; and in the absence of that WHY the evidence from Motivational Mapping in mapping tens of thousands of individuals is that the organisation cannot succeed in the long-run if they do not take into account the WHY, since so many of its employees crave the purpose or meaning of what they are trying to do.

Third,[10] the 'hygiene factors' that we alluded to previously now come to the fore. We note that three motivators in particular Friend (ranked 7th), Director (ranked 8th), and Star (ranked 9th and lowest in all 10 sectors) do not appear in any of the sectors' top three motivators. What are the implications of this? Well, we have already seen in Chapter 3 how the Friend motivator might be exactly the perspective we need to adopt in understanding the customer. The absence of the Director motivator seems almost equally worrying in that it is the Achievement motivator par excellence, and yet it is not one that is really firing up many managers: they are doing the job or fulfilling the role for other motivational reasons, but this can easily lead to a shortfall in how the job is being done. Finally, the universally low scoring of the Star motivator is deeply concerning as recognition is at the heart of it.

That individuals are not on the one hand seeking personal recognition may sound altruistic, but is it actually realistic? Virtually all authorities agree that recognition is essential[11] if people are to flourish; it's a primary relationship motivator – it's about gaining strength, as it were, from others who acknowledge us.

What this third point leads to is a need for organisations and teams to review three key areas: 1) how communications occur within the organisation/ team and with a special focus on the sense of belonging that the Friend motivator drives; 2) how management operates and how managers are selected and developed within organisations and teams, or the Director motivator; and 3) how recognition is attributed and awarded with organisations and teams, and how much focus there is on it. Interestingly, the Friend and Star motivators are both Relationship-driven, and Relationship-driven motivators are bound up with helping the customer. Thus, we return in a way to our preoccupation in Chapter 3 with the customer.

Let's take the 'What We Do' from Figure 3.8, and based on what we have said above expand it further in Figure 4.3.

We see from this the centrality of the Why or purpose around the customer. Also, we are driven to ask how we do what do: what activities and delivery methods do we use? Here we are essentially also asking, how do we perform when we do this? And our performance crucially leads us back to considering the skills, knowledge and motivations of our staff. Finally, we see the What – our products and services – also needing to have a customer focus too; we have to ask, what do we supply? And, who is this for? And, of course, do or will they want it? As we ask that question, we are immediately into the realm of strategy[12] for the organisation: how do we differentiate[13] our offering, what is our unique selling proposition, or why should the customer buy from us? But note the strange paradox of considering what we

Figure 4.3 What We Do: Why, How and What

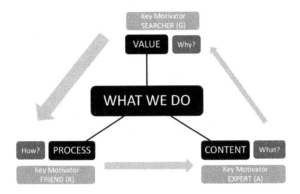

Figure 4.4 What We Do: Value, Process, and Content

do, and what we do derives from two points more primary: why we do it and how we do it!

What we have, then, from this is something like Figure 4.4.

If we study this, we realise that determining what we do is not just a simple question of saying I intend to sell mobile phones or houses or panini or beer – to illustrate services as well as products – or surveying or nursing or coaching or teaching. On the contrary, what we do is framed in the first instance by Why we are doing it. This will almost certainly be a value that we attach great importance to. In motivational terms the ultimate 'why' motivator – the key motivator – is the Searcher, for why we are doing anything is ultimately to make a difference. To phrase this slightly differently: we can make a difference, but sadly this difference can be a negative one; what we are seeking, if we are psychologically healthy, is to improve the life of the customer in some fundamental way. This is true even at the level of a supermarket selling bread[14]: whilst it is true that the customer may not see buying the bread so much as an improvement but more as a necessity, the point remains relevant.

Activity 4.3

To labour the issue, perhaps, but how would you make the case for buying bread in a supermarket as being an improvement in the life of the customer?

In the first instance, the customer is given a choice of breads, and so is able to choose their 'preferred' bread, which perceptually may be an issue of quality or cost, but either way benefits the customer's life. Second, although bread may be regarded as a need, its absence leads to a form of hygiene factor: we take it for granted till we don't have it, and then we realise how important it is to our lives.[15] Third, properly understood, the bread is beneficial to our lives in the sense of its potential taste and freshness, as well as the nutrients it supplies us with. For these reasons alone, then, we can see that the selling of anything or everything is about adding some perceived improvement to the life, experience or situation of the customer.[16] Hence why the Searcher motivator is the key motivator here, for it could be said to underpin all transactions; and at their best, the purchases may be transformational for the customer and the supplier.

However, all the motivators offer clues as to the WHY we do what we do. Figure 4.5 sets out a table with some information regarding the contributions each motivator is likely to make; and also supplying some sector examples of where this particular WHY might be extremely prominent or operative.

Before discussing Figure 4.5 a number of points need to be clarified. First, motivators are internal drives – energies if you will – but in seeking, say, freedom or autonomy for ourselves (Spirit) we tend to project them outwards and assume or even want them for others. So with all the motivators: our own energies drive us to build a world based around them, and as we have said in previous books these become values for us.[17]

Second, we must note that motivators can and do interact; but for the ease of simplicity, and because in Figure 4.2 we presented a ranking based on the top motivator only, it is best to consider them in isolation. That said, an organisation may have a complex series of WHYs, though as with values – which are always hierarchical – there will always be a root reason

Motivator	Motivator 'Why'	Typical Sector Examples
Searcher: Key	Improve for customer life, experiences or situations	Charities
Spirit	Improve for customer autonomy, decision-making or time utilisation	Information Technologies
Creator	Improve for customer cost, speed or quality	Pharmaceuticals
Expert: Key	Improve for customer expertise, knowledge or skills	Education Sector
Builder	Improve for customer utility, competitiveness or profitability	Financial Services
Director	Improve for customer control, management or effectiveness	Property Sector
Star	Improve for customer recognition, importance or status	Marketing and PR
Friend: Key	Improve for customer community, belonging or relationships	Voluntary Sector
Defender	Improve for customer reliability, value-for-money or efficiency	Public Sector

Figure 4.5 Motivator WHYs

why we are doing what we do. And connected to this, it is important to stress that when we instance the typical sectors, we are not implying that the sector examples are rigidly in just one category. Apple Inc., for example, may well produce many products that increase its clients' autonomy, decision-making capabilities and time utilisation (Spirit); but they also improve customer status (Star – the caché of owning an Apple); situations (Searcher – the experience of owning Apple products); and competitiveness (Builder – their effectiveness demonstrated in many ways, including their interactivity). Indeed, some might argue that I have got it all wrong with Apple: certainly, Spirit is important for them – they have always been a sort of maverick, go their own way, kind of company – but perhaps their Creator or Expert dimensions are more important?

Whatever the reality is with Apple let others who are more informed decide. However, it is important to remember that motivators change over time: a snapshot of Apple in 1990, 2000, 2010 and now (2020) might reveal four very different companies from a motivational perspective. And what we are saying about Apple – which we have placed in the IT (Spirit) category – applies to all the sector examples: any particular case may appear in another motivational category at any point in time. The important thing to consider about any company is whether its WHY is aligned with its motivators

Finally, on Figure 4.5 I have identified three motivators as 'Key' and to do this I have selected one motivator from each of the three primary groupings of RAG. What I am highlighting here is what I consider root motivators in terms of the WHY. Obviously, Searcher is at the forefront because, as we have said, making a difference is quite directly a WHY issue; also, it is by far and away the most common motivator to be ranked first. Thus, top performing teams need to consider this issue as they develop their Remit.

Expert is ranked second. We are in a knowledge economy[18]; we cannot help but see that the old ways of doing things are rapidly becoming obsolescent, and that new knowledge, new skills, are driving change forward. Employees, as Figure 4.2 shows, want this and are motivated by it. In a way, then, for top performing teams this becomes a question of asking: What do we need to know and what skills do we need to have to be effective? Are we motivated to learn?

Finally, I have included the Friend motivator as Key, although unlike the Searcher and Expert, which are first and second in the rankings in Figure 4.2, it is apparently only 7th in importance for employees. The natural 'Key' motivator from the R type motivators would appear to be the Defender, which is ranked 4th and appears almost three times more frequently than the Friend as number one motivator in staff profiles. However, though security and stability may be a more deeply rooted motivator than belonging and friendship in terms of the Maslow Hierarchy, at a truly WHY level the Friend motivator is the one that holds the key to long-term success for a team (or an organisation). What is the reason for this?

Activity 4.4

Review the materials we have covered in Chapters 3 and 4. Think about what the Defender and Friend motivators are essentially about and then answer the question – why is it that for long-term team and organisational success we might be better-off keeping in mind the Friend motivator rather than the Defender? List some of your reasons.

The reasons are actually many and various. Firstly, it is good to remember what we established in Chapter 1 about what a team is. It had four characteristics, two of which are highly pertinent here (see Figure 1.1): namely, interdependency and strong belief. This latter characteristic specifically included a strong belief in the power of the team itself. Interdependency was about belonging and co-operation (Figure 1.2) and strong beliefs meant that the acronym T.E.A.M. was alive and well: Together Each Achieves More. Essentially, these are processes within the team rather than the content of what the team is striving to achieve. Therefore, top performing teams must cultivate that sense of belonging whether the Friend motivator is in the top three or not; and we know that it is frequently not.

Top Motivator
Second Motivator
Third Motivator
Lowest Motivator

Team Motivation Score: 76%

Change Index Score: 62

RAG: 31-33-36

Name	Searcher	Expert	Defender	Creator	Builder	Spirit	Star	Director	Friend	%	Motivation Audit 1	2	3
Sam	27	30	17	17	25	17	12	25	10	100%	10	10	10
Joe	24	16	18	25	19	16	22	25	15	97%	10	9	10
Ellie	28	23	25	26	15	11	22	18	12	90%	9	9	9
Linda	37	24	25	24	13	21	8	15	13	100%	10	10	10
Barbara	27	21	22	20	20	21	17	15	17	82%	8	9	7
Lawrence	29	28	19	29	9	11	20	17	18	74%	8	6	8
Paul	24	20	21	18	20	22	17	18	20	65%	8	5	2
Jon	20	33	25	20	18	16	15	16	17	91%	10	7	10
Janet	27	21	28	22	21	18	13	9	21	86%	9	8	8
Dan Johnson	20	22	25	14	20	22	24	19	14	25%	3	1	4
Pete	24	19	22	18	22	18	17	21	19	76%	8	7	7
Josh	21	21	22	20	25	20	18	20	13	45%	2	8	9
Ivan	16	7	13	26	17	30	30	24	17	51%	4	6	9
Keith	28	21	20	24	21	16	22	9	19	61%	6	6	7
Andrew	26	25	25	14	19	20	17	17	17	90%	9	9	9
Total	378	331	327	317	284	279	274	268	242	76%			

Figure 4.6 Team Map with Friend lowest

Before considering some other reasons why the Friend motivator is a Key motivator for high performing teams, let's consider a team map where Friend really is the lowest!

This Map is from a highly successful company with some 20 or so distribution premises in major towns and cities across the UK. This Map reflects one of the centres which comprises a retail outlet together with an IT sales force. In other words, it is predominantly a sales team with administrative back-up staff included in the profile.

Activity 4.5

Given our topic, what three germane things might you comment on, based on this Map?

First, the Friend motivator is not just the lowest motivator,[19] but is by far and away the lowest motivator; at 242 it is well below the Director at 268, whereas the Director is only 6 points behind the Star at 274. Second, 4 people out of 15 have it as their lowest motivator and to compound the issue only 2 people have a score for the Friend of 20 or above (the 'above' here is only 21). Since below 20 means that the motivator has less pull or effect, we can assume that hardly anyone in this team is really bothered about belonging to it! Third, though the Team Motivation Score seems relatively high (76%), we have Dan who is only 25%.

And why is Dan's score significant? It is because of the PMA scores that go with it: we see that he may have a low motivational score partly because two (Spirit and Star) of his top three motivators are out of sync with rest of the team's and, furthermore, we find that his PMA scoring for the top three motivators is very revealing: Defender (3/10), Star (1/10), Spirit (4/10). It is the Star score that is so startling: this is a Relationship motivator, like the Friend, and it involves perceived recognition, and he has scored it 1/10. At this point it is appropriate to seek more information in constructing our top performing team. In fact, we should look at Dan's full 22 numbers, and doing so we find the following in Figure 4.7.

In building a top performing team by using motivational profiles, we now come to very advanced understandings of the motivators, and in particular, how they interact. Before commenting on it, try to work out for yourself what is going on here and why it is significant.

Activity 4.6

Study Dan's 22 numbers in Figure 4.7 with particular reference to his PMA scores out of 10. To add a little context, Dan is a manager within this team and is in fact a high performing member of it. Given this, what then emerges from these numbers?

Analysis for Dan Johnson - Sheffield		
Raw Results		
Motivator	Score	PMA Score / 10
Defender	25	3
Star	24	1
Spirit	22	4
Expert	22	9
Builder	20	3
Searcher	20	10
Director	19	9
Creator	14	8
Friend	14	3
PMA Score	25%	
Cluster Importance		
Relationship (R)		35%
Achievement (A)		34%
Growth (G)		31%

Figure 4.7 Dan's 22 numbers

The PMA score of 25%, an exceptionally low score and one placing Dan in the Action Zone, is based on an algorithm which only takes into account the top three motivators. From a team perspective – though not from a coaching one – we don't need to look at all the nine PMA scores. But here we see quite a remarkable thing: the top three motivators along with his remuneration (Builder 3/10) and sense of belonging (Friend 3/10) are clearly unmet. But – and a very big BUT – three motivators which are not so important to him are very clearly satisfied: his Expert motivator (9/10) is very high, his Searcher, making a difference for the customer is an extraordinary 10/10! And he is a manager, and he clearly feels that he is managing well, with his Director motivator at 9/10. Indeed, the overall scoring of the team also suggests he is managing well, since they are 76% motivated, and that suggests too that his levels of expertise are high.

But notice further this: two motivators that are not so significant to him (though Expert is 4th with a score of 22/40 and hence does have some traction for him) are the top two motivators of the whole team. In other words – and as happened – Dan seems to be performing at a high level in those very areas in which the whole team wants to perform; and, additionally, he has managing drives which more generally are lacking within the rest of the team. Thus, Dan seems to compensate for a profound lack of motivation in other team members.

What is this upshot of this? First, that until the Motivational Maps were completed, no-one had any idea that their manager was demotivated! He seemed to be motivated in those very areas in which they were too. And, equally, if belonging wasn't important to him, neither was it to them. But that would be a misreading, for what the Map is actually revealing, and which proved true, is that either Dan was heading for a health or wellness issue as he struggled to conceal his true feelings – and motivators; or, Dan would be heading the stress off at the pass, as it were, by contemplating quitting the role. This proved to be exactly what he was thinking of.

But, still more, notice that Dan's top two motivators are both Relationship-driven, even if Friend is not one of them (the R is highest at 35% in the Cluster Importance). The reality here is that Friend is a definite and dangerous hygiene factor for the whole team, but especially for Dan. In some curious way Dan is the motivational flip-side of his own team; he is the motivational 'diversity' that leads to the team having a massive strength and range. Yes, the team is all set to make a difference, prove their expertise to the customer, and so on; but Dan, first and foremost, wants to get things right, wants the systems to be efficient, and the processes smooth and predictable (Defender). This is a counter balance to the Searcher, and as the leader this was proving extremely effective. But there is a toll on Dan – which the scores show.

Indeed, the second motivator, Star, says it all: he scores his satisfaction with this the lowest of all, 1 out of 10, though it is Dan's second most important motivator. It would be true to say here that precisely because Star is the most frequently identified lowest motivator, it can have a bad 'rap'. By this I mean that the highly motivated Star can to other types appear ego-driven, narcissistic and rampantly self-obsessed. This is extremely unfair. Of course, a Star-motivated individual with low self-esteem will exhibit behaviour that is negative; but this is true of all the motivators – they have the potential when self-esteem is low to reveal their 'dark' or more negative side. But where we have someone with moderate to high levels of self-esteem the desire for recognition is healthy too.

And here's the interesting point: where the self-esteem is low, there will not be enough recognition to go round, and so the Star-motivated type will withhold it from others. But where the self-esteem is healthy, the Star type will do what all the types do at that level: namely, project it out. The Searcher, for example, in wanting to make a difference, will seek out others and want them to make a difference too; or, the Expert will admire and seek out others with expertise. So Dan, in this instance, was a manager giving out recognition relentlessly to his staff, but his own craving for it, especially from his own company bosses, was not being met.

The top performing team here, then, is precarious, since its manager is not being fed with the motivational fuel he needs, and although belonging is not one of his motivators, Dan is quite clear that he isn't being made to feel he belongs. It should not be difficult to see that there is a link here between the Star and Friend motivators; they are both Relationship driven, and moreover taking the time to enable Dan to feel he belongs is an important form of recognition. Feeding the one may well fuel the other. At the heart of this is understanding how the top team works within itself, and from outside too. In essence they are both about that fundamental way in which people – employees – feel important; we make them feel important, or not. To belong is to be important, and this links with Figure 1.1 again and interdependency; and to give recognition is usually to make someone feel they belong.

So, as I develop these points, we come to re-visiting Activity 4.4. Figure 1.1 gives interdependency and strong belief in the efficacy of teams as reasons why. We have partially covered aspects of the interdependency even at the motivational levels, and at the level of process. So far as belief goes, the belief is in T.E.A.M: an acronym[20] standing for Together Each Achieves More. Belief creates expectancy and expectancy often becomes a self-fulfilling prophecy.

But perhaps as important as all these answers are, there is yet another: nobody, it is claimed,[21] on their death bed says, 'I wish I'd spent more time in the office'! On the contrary, virtually everyone says, 'I'd wish I'd spent more time with my family, my loved ones and friends'. More generally, one is reminded of the philosopher Bertrand Russell's observation[22]: 'One of the symptoms of approaching nervous breakdown is the belief that one's work is terribly important, and that to take a holiday would bring all kinds of disaster. If I were a medical man, I should prescribe a holiday to any patient who considered his work important'. The obsession with work – with the big A of Achievement – has a dark downside: stress, burnout and illness. People are one of the significant antidotes – through strong, positive relationships.

Activity 4.7 (Activity 4.4 revisited)

Now consider what we have covered so far. Think about what the Defender and Friend motivators are essentially about and then answer the question – why is it that for long-term team and organisational success we might be better-off keeping in mind the Friend motivator rather than the Defender? List some of your reasons.

The need for security is a normal and healthy human desire, so let's be clear about that; but also I think if we reflect on it at any length, we can immediately see that it is the obverse side of that chronic and debilitating emotion we call fear. Ultimately, the lack of security prompts in us feelings of fear and we do everything in our power to counteract that fear. In terms of the Defender motivator, this counteraction tends to focus on creating stable structures, systems and processes in which results – future outcomes – become more highly predictable,[23] thus reducing fear. This is good, so far as it goes, but we mustn't forget that the emotion of fear can blind us to reality and lead to less than optimum decisions.

Conversely, whilst the need to belong is also a normal and healthy human desire, its obverse side (where not co-dependent) generates the emotion we call love. And love is the antidote to fear.[24] So if we think about this from a top performing team's perspective, the belonging (ie Friend) motivator is a kind of glue that holds people together, that resists fear and its weak decision-making, and provides an additional energy that comes from a belief and a commitment to each other.[25]

To expand this further: fear's response to threat tends to focus on legislation, contracts, remuneration, property, pensions and all the other paraphernalia of 'things'[26] we seek to acquire; these can never provide true security.[27] But belonging provides much deeper and long-lasting satisfactions. Hence people want to spend more time with those they love; and from a work perspective, they enjoy going to work! Moreover, not only do they like work because they like being there, but they also become more productive as a result. We need to remember that the essence of selling itself – and everyone, as Brian Tracy observed,[28] is in selling whatever their role – is KLT[29]: the customer must Know you first, then Like you second, and then if they Trust you too, they will want to buy from you! It should be evident that the getting to *like* you is inherent in 'liking' someone, and when we belong we tend to like our associates!

As Dr Tom Malone observed,[30] 'The hard stuff is easy. The soft stuff is hard. And the soft stuff is a lot more important than the hard stuff'. This is the challenge, since we are dealing not just with motivation, which is itself part of the 'soft' stuff, but belonging and friendship and the glue that makes people want to work together and perform.

Activity 4.8

Imagine you have teams or even a team in which the Friend motivator is low or even the lowest motivator. Remember, that belonging will not seem important to them, but you know that without that sense of belonging, the team is likely to fragment or burn-out. What three or four Reward Strategies might you begin to adopt that could perhaps subtly bring in a greater sense of togetherness?

Context is everything, so what may work in one organisation may not in another. But some great ideas to consider are given in Figure 4.8. Try one or two of the ideas in Figure 4.8. Strive to make 'What You Do' a process that binds people together as well as being goal orientated. Further Team Rewards for the Friend are to be found in the Resources section.

We move now in Chapter 5 to the third and final component of The Remit: Values we insist on.

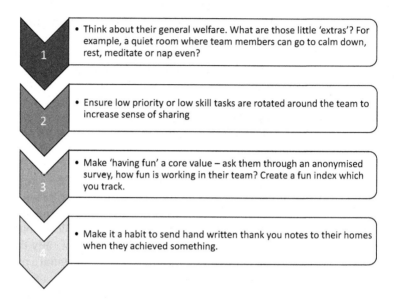

Figure 4.8 Activating more belonging (Friend) for top performing teams

Notes

1 And here we must put in a caveat in that in the last 5 years the wellness issue of employees has steadily risen up the priority chart of employer concerns, and with this has come the increasing recognition that people do not come to work just to make a wage.

2 'People work for money, but die for a cause', said an anonymous CEO: cited by James Pickford, *Mastering Management 2.0: Your Single-source Guide to Becoming a Master of Management* (Pearson Education, 2001).

3 The word for this might be managerialism, which is defined as a belief in or reliance on the use of professional managers in administering or planning an activity.

4 Research done by Motivational Maps Ltd on a cross-section of over 100 sectors with over 13,000 maps in 2017 found an average of 39.5% individuals who had Searcher as their number one motivator. This is extraordinarily high; the second ranking motivator was the Expert where some 14.4% had it as their number one motivator. The lowest was the Star with only 1.1% having it as number one. Since Searcher can often be in opposition to Builder (but not always), the notion that simply leveraging money as a way of motivating staff, given the high levels of Searcher, is absurd. Indeed, these statistics alone suggest why there is such demotivation and disengagement in those organisations where a Builder mentality dominates all proceedings.

5 See *Mapping Motivation*, James Sale (Routledge, 2016), Chapter 4 for more on hygiene factors. Essentially, these are the lowest motivators which we tend to ignore, but which can become an Achilles' heel in any enterprise we undertake, whether individually, at team or organisational levels.

6   Thanks here to Dr Shirley Thompson who did the data analytics to make this possible. See https://bit.ly/2wgUYct

7   Writing in the *Financial Times*, DHL CEO, Frank Appel, maintained that 'when goals are predominantly financial, purpose is often lost'. He adds, therefore, two items to the bottom line: employee satisfaction and environmental targets. It appears to be working: staff surveys show workers feel more motivated than when he took over in 2009, and the company's revenues have climbed from Euro 53bn in 2011 to an expected Euro 60bn in 2017. Cited in Patrick McGee, *MoneyWeek*, 2/2/2018.

8   David McNally's expression perhaps nails why: 'Growth and contribution are our primary mission in life', from *Even Eagles Need A Push* (Penguin, 1994).

9   Simon Sinek, *Start With the Why* (Penguin, 2009).

10 As always with Maps, there are many more points that could be analysed and discussed. Here for example, that not only Builder, but also Creator also only appears once. Given the significance of Creator generally in terms of organisational innovation, that is an issue. As is the question of the motivators that appear which may be in opposition: Spirit and Defender is one good example. Readers may wish to reflect on what this might mean or betoken.

11 'There's a tight coupling between results, compensation, and recognition' – Gary Hamel, *The Future of Management* (Harvard Business School Press, 2007).

12 The complexity in today's world cannot be overemphasised. A company like Macdonald's might seem to be company which sells hamburgers, but in fact they make more money through their property; Coca-Cola's prime business is 'selling rights to other firms which make, bottle and sell its drink'. And Apple doesn't manufacture a single phone! – Ed Conway, The Times, The Huge Profits in Thin Air, cited *MoneyWeek*, 14/02/2020.

13 'Put all your energy and resources into areas where you are substantially different from any rival', Richard Koch, *The 80/20 Principle and 92 Other Powerful Laws of Nature* (Nicolas Brealey, 2014).

14 There is a spiritual sidebar to mention here. For in the Bible it is written that 'man shall not live by bread alone'. The benefits of bread are clearly implied in the word 'alone' – yes, there may be something more important than physical bread, but bread certainly is necessary. If we complete the quotation – found in the Old and New Testaments (Deuteronomy 8: 2–3 and Matthew 4:4, King James Version) we find 'Man shall not live by bread alone, but by every word that proceedeth out of the mouth of God'. This 'every word … out of the mouth of God' may be viewed as the 'meaning' or purpose of life; in other words, the higher calling. Put another way, we are not just animals who need to eat, but human beings who need to have a meaning in life. This correlates with our Searcher motivator and the highest level of Maslow's Hierarchy where we self-actualise.

15 As G.K. Chesterton observed: 'When it comes to life, the critical thing is whether you take things for granted or take them with gratitude'. From *Irish Impressions* (IHS Press, 2002), originally published 1919.

16 Including purchasing if only to get the vendor off our back or case!

17 See especially, *Mapping Motivation for Coaching*, James Sale and Bevis Moynan (Routledge, 2018), Chapter 7.

18 Perhaps one of the best examples of the exponential change that is engulfing us is referred to in Ross Thornley's book, *Moonshot Innovation* (CrunchX Ltd., 2019) where he cites Peter Diamandis' The Six Ds of exponential technology: Digitization, Deception, Disruption, Dematerialisation, Demonetisation, and Democratisation. These are drivers of change and basically they affect

everything in our society and our world. As a 'given', then, the need for increasing expertise is almost self-evident.

19   And notice too that the order is Searcher and Expert as first and second; again,
another example of the prevalence of these motivators.

20   For more on this see James Sale, *Mapping Motivation*, ibid., Chapter 6.

21   'Nobody on their deathbed has ever said "I wish I had spent more time at the
office"' – attributed to Rabbi Harold Kushner or sometimes to Senator Paul
Tsongas.

22   Bertrand Russell, *The Conquest of Happiness* (1930; republished Liveright
Publishing Corporation, 2013).

23   'The risk you should worry most about is the risk of not taking risks', Richard
Koch, ibid.

24   John Mark Green, for example, says: 'If you want to tap into what life has to
offer, let love be your primary mode of being, not fear. Fear closes us down and
makes us retreat. It locks doors and limits opportunities. Love is about opening
to possibilities. Seeing the world with new eyes. It widens our heart and mind.
Fear incarcerates, but love liberates' – https://bit.ly/30RWn5V

25   Of course, the inability to belong may cause fear as well, but I am highlighting
here a contrast. It would be true to say as well that the need for security naturally leads to belonging, since we are never as secure as when we belong; so in
that sense the Defender and Friend are complementary, not antagonistic to each
other. But Maslow observed that, 'In any given moment, we have two options: to
step forward into growth or to step back into safety'. Defender activities where
we step back and try to reduce insecurity via 'things' and processes may be
thought of as feared based; whereas, Defender activities that step forward into
building relationships, belonging, and teams, can be thought of as the way of
love and growth.

26   For an extended treatise on the difference between people and things, see
Chapter 8 of *Mapping Motivation for Leadership*, ibid.

27   'Remind yourself that the search for certainty won't get you anywhere, so it's
important to consciously shift your attention away from that futile vortex' –
Beatrice Chestnut, *The Complete Enneagram* (She Writes Press, 2013).

28   Brian Tracy, *Advanced Selling Strategies* (Simon & Schuster, 1995).

29   Jeremy Marchant, *Network Better: How to Meet, Connect & Grow Your Business*
(Practical Inspiration Publishing, 2018).

30   Dr Tom Malone, President and CEO, Milliken & Company, cited in *1001 Ways
to Energize Employees*, Bob Nelson (Workman Publishing, 1997).

Chapter 5

Getting to The Remit

Values We Insist On

At this point we need a brief recap. We established in Chapter 3 that establishing the Remit was central to a high performing team. The problem with this idea is that The Remit, despite being a short word of only five letters, is not an easy 'thing' to determine; that in fact there are three key dimensions of The Remit, and they are in a dynamic tension with each other. Readers of other books in our Mapping Motivation series will realise that this is not an uncommon phenomenon in mapping. For example, motivation itself is the product of three interacting and dynamic sources (see Figure 2.5); and, furthermore, even the nine motivators themselves are in three dynamic clusters – the RAG – which are not discrete, but rather holistic in how they affect each other (see Figure S.1).

Thus, although The Remit pitches this interactivity to a new level of complexity, in essence it is something we are familiar with and should welcome. The Remit is What We Do, but this is not a matter we can consider in isolation, but only with respect to the customer (HOW) and the values that drive us (WHY) (see Figure 3.8). Unsurprisingly, because this is tripartite in nature, then it follows the Law of Three.[1] This law is too big an issue to cover now, but one important point to note is that wherever the Law of Three operates, something new comes into existence.[2] Two forces cancel each other out, and so no progress is made; but the introduction of the third force produces a new resolution, something different, or put another way, the Law of Three is integral to all change.

Activity 5.1

What is the most practical application of the Law of Three as outlined above to The Remit?

This means – in practical terms – that no establishment of The Remit can be considered final; it will always be changing, not necessarily every five minutes, but certainly every few years, if not sooner, and we will need to review it. Indeed, every top performing will have it on its agenda to discuss at least once every year. And this makes sense, for think about it: all three components of The Remit can or may change over time. Certainly, and first of all, the Customer Focus is likely to produce new demands and needs of the customer, which will almost certainly affect what we do; conversely, what we do – a new product or service offering – may well alter the customer's perspective or demand on us. Values can also evolve and improve over time,[3] although some values may be timeless: for example, a value such as – if we included it – 'honesty' might never change; but others can, or new ones may be added or even some removed.

With these points in mind, we recall that we looked at the Customer Focus in Chapter 3 and What We Do in Chapter 4. These are essentially notes and tools on what to look for as one builds a top performing team, and especially, as is our interest, with regard to motivation. Now we need to consider the Values We Insist On, the third element. We provided some useful techniques on this in two of our previous books,[4] including the correlation of motivators with potential values, positive and negative aspects of the values, and how beliefs and values lead to our choices. Clearly, we don't want to just repeat that material, and so we refer interested readers to it; but values and motivation are two aspects of work and our lives that need constant attention, and we need a range of tools and techniques with which to examine what is going on.

One of the most powerful tools that we have developed in Mapping Motivation, and which is an intrinsic component of our Motivational Organisational Map is what we call Measuring the PMV scores.[5] This is going to take some unpacking, but we think the effort is worth it, since like the Map itself it provides so much rich information.

What, then, is the PMV score and why is this so important for top performing teams and as a tool for management to develop top performing teams? The first thing to mention almost by way of passing is that the Motivational Map is a self-perception inventory tool; in other words, that in completing a map one is comparing oneself with oneself and not with another individual or against a standard. So, self-assessment or self-rating is something that Maps find highly congenial. In a different way, the PMV score is another kind of self-rating.[6]

We think, for all its obvious subjectivity, that self-rating tends to be accurate except mainly when two unfortunate situations appertain. Self-rating can be inaccurate and misleading when either the self-rater is (1) in a state of fear[7] – for example, they are afraid of what their manager might think of the result. Or (2), the reverse – they suffer from a sort of false modesty and a false belief that no one can be a 10/10 because 'there is always room for improvement' syndrome.[8] In the former case, the self-rater will tend to over-score themselves: in the Maps we see this when we find, for example, PMA scores of 10 for all nine motivators – what chance is it that anybody could really be 10/10 for all nine motivators, including their lowest? Here is someone wishing to appear 'motivated' to their manager and not taking any chances as to what their scoring might be. Of course, the false result betrays itself and provides an opportunity for a deeper look at the intrinsic issue within the team.

The latter situation tends to lead to underscoring: the individual does not give themselves enough credit for that they have done, or even how they feel. This is more difficult to detect immediately as an erroneous result, but from a management perspective in building a team, it is more desirable than the first situation – it is much easier to build someone up when it is apparent that they are performing at a higher level than they think than it is to uncover and deal with deception. In Map terms we tend to find that those operating with a 'always room for improvement' mentality are more frequently encountered at the operational level, whereas the 'afraid of what the manager thinks' is more at the middle management level – those aspiring to get to senior levels and for whom their bosses' good opinions are vital.

These two exceptions are not the norm. However, we need to be aware of them when we look at the PMV process so that we do not accept results uncritically. Remember: perfection is the enemy of progress – we are not looking for perfect results, but useful ones on which we can take practical action steps. As they say in NLP (Neuro Linguistic Programming), the map is not the territory, which means that all models are imprecise in some way; what we have with the PMV scores is a model that is highly useful.

The starting point for considering PMV scores is to take all or some of the teams within an organisation and compare them based along four key elements of their existence. Figure 5.1 shows six teams, starting with the

Measuring Team PMV* Scores				
	Motivation %	Productivity / 10	Manageability / 10	Contribution to Org Values / 10
Board				
Senior Management				
Finance				
Sales				
Marketing				
Operations				
TOTAL				
AVERAGE				

Figure 5.1 Team PMV scores for an organisation
PMV* scoring is for each team in each category out of 10, where 10 is outstanding and 1 is very poor.

Board of the organisation, considered as a team itself, down to the Operations team. We can fine-tune this analysis by either removing or adding teams as we or management see fit.

Activity 5.2

Without further explanation on my part, and assuming that the headings are virtually self-explanatory (although we shall still go on to explain them!), consider any team that you are either in or can observe first hand in your organisation, and score them. It would be particularly insightful and useful if you were able to compare your scores for the team that you are in (you may manage) and to set these alongside a team that you know well in the same organisation, or even perhaps a team you were in before your current post. As a first stab, what do you learn or notice about your team or the other team you have scored?

The first score in the Motivation column is the score from the Team Motivational Map. This will be a percentage score which for the purposes of comparison with the other PMV scores we can turn into a score out of 10, either rounding up or down according to the normal arithmetical rules: so 76% would become 7.6 or 8 out of 10, whereas 75% would be 7.5 or 7.

Before, looking at best methods to generate meaningful data here, let's consider the column headings and what they mean and might reveal to us.

Most obviously – and as the foundation as it were – we want to know is the team motivated, and at what level? We then have the PMV criteria. These are: How Productive (P) is this Team? How easy to Manage (M) is this Team? And how much does this Team contribute to Organisational values (V)? Note that in this instance we have not included our old favourite P – as in P for performance – partly because it is more directly correlated with motivation, as we have discussed at length in our earlier books, and partly because at the end of the day organisations want the productivity that results from high level performance. Indeed, productivity is the issue of our times nationally[9] and internationally.

But just being motivated and productive are not enough, at least for a top performing team; there is more. We think that there are two other vital dimensions to consider: manageability and, our old friend, values! Let's look at all three dimensions in a little more detail.

First, productivity. In the normal course of events, productivity and motivation should go hand in hand. That is, highly motivated staff should be highly productive. Alternatively, if your staff are poorly motivated and productivity is not high, that should come as no surprise either. We talk of Reward Strategies to motivate employees and teams in order to increase productivity. But what if motivation is high but productivity is low, or productivity is high and motivation is low? These would be counterintuitive results but not entirely unusual. It is possible for staff to be productive but not motivated – at least, for a while. In these situations, one needs to investigate the causes carefully. Some possible reasons for high motivation and low productivity are: lack of skills or knowledge, unanticipated implementation problems, absence of appropriate leadership, flawed strategies, system failures, poor communications and inadequate planning. Some possible reasons for low motivation and high productivity are: insufficient involvement of those affected, fear, economic or cultural climate, focus on things and not people,[10] over-competitiveness. Although the latter problem seems less problematic than the former, high productivity in the long run is not sustainable with a demotivated workforce; for one thing, staff leave as soon as that option becomes tenable. The question, then, is how productive are your team? We know how motivated they are through Motivational Maps.

Second, manageability. This is a word we like to use to describe the process of running, or managing or leading a team; the key word here is 'process'. How easy a team is to manage is also an important issue to consider when dealing with them and considering their value to the organisation. Ever had a customer who spends money with you but is hellishly diffcult to service?

Activity 5.3

Think about a very difficult client or customer you have had in your working experience. What was he or she or the organisation itself like? What problems did this cause for you, your team or your business? How did you resolve this? And finally, knowing what you now know, and if you did a cost-benefit analysis, was having the customer really worth it? What would you do differently, knowing what you now know?

Staff, and teams, can be just like that difficult customer, and sometimes we have to ask whether the value of the team outweighs the problems they may cause. To take two examples at different ends of the motivational spectrum: the Spirit team may be persistently difficult to manage at all; whereas the Friend team may be too dependent on direction and coaxing. The key thing is the fit of the team leader and their style of leadership with the team profile. Thus a team's motivation needs to be considered alongside their manageability: if they are highly motivated but not easily manageable, then why is that? Do the motivators themselves tell us anything? Conversely, if motivation is low but they are easily manageable what is that saying? Probably, that they are marking time and not optimising performance (so time to compare the productivity too). And again, if they are poorly motivated and not easily manageable, that makes sense – but what to do about it? What, then, does contrasting manageability against productivity reveal?

Figure 5.2 shows us the likely scenarios in each of the four possible quadrants. Regarding the Dysfunctional quadrant, it may result from a clash of

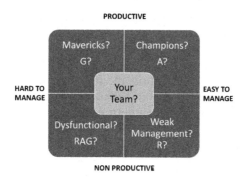

Figure 5.2 Manageability versus Productivity quadrants

competing motivators, or even similar motivators whereby, for example, too many Directors or too many Stars are competing for space. But at its root, it is not the motivators causing the problem: it is the low self-esteem of the team members and/or bad leadership that compounds the problem. At that level the motivators, whilst true, become irrelevant: the wants of the motivators have been replaced by the more basic needs for survival and security. Dealing with such a team almost invariably requires somebody outside the team seeing it objectively for what it is, and then taking decisive action.

As for the Weak Management quadrant, we have here what potentially we can classify as the Country Club style of management. Here, everyone is comfortable, no-one wants to rock the boat, and the expression 'jobs for life' springs to mind. There is little change or innovation, for 'Good ideas and solid concepts have a great deal of difficulty in being understood by those who earn their living by doing it some other way'.[11] This can be, though not always, motivationally driven: the motivators most *likely* to result in comfort and change resistance will be especially the Relationship motivators.[12] If we do identify a team as being in this quadrant, then this is an important clue to look for in the motivational profile.

By contrast, the Maverick team, which is highly productive, will certainly have a high motivational root cause, and the most likely scenario for this will be a motivational Growth orientation. And one of the reasons they will be hard to manage is to do with the properties of Growth motivators: namely, their future orientation. In dealing with the future one is always wrestling with uncertainty and ambiguity; and this requires non-standard methodologies for coping with and dealing with 'things'. Hence, we inevitably have to have maverick-type people who can endure this lack of certainty, this more fluid scenario. Obviously, the Spirit motivator is by its very nature not easily manageable, but it's not easy either to manage 'creatives', for creativity can lead anyone away from the official 'script'. And Searchers too can be value-driven to make that *real* difference in a manner that can override the overt and espoused values of the team or organisation.

Finally, the Champions, the dream as it were of all organisations: highly productive teams who are highly manageable. Management gets the productivity they want with the lowest amount of effort and stress involved. Champions can be any combination of motivators, so it is important to emphasize there is no stereotyping here. But all things being equal, the Achievement motivator types are more likely to occupy this space: unencumbered in some respects by loyalty to each other, less troubled by visions of the future, they have a job to do in the present: to get management and levels of control right, to be competitive and to be best, and to be experts – deep experts – at what they do.

Activity 5.4

Study Figure 5.2. Consider any team that you have been a member of or have managed or led. In which quadrant would they be? What quadrant might be the best one for them and the organisation? What steps do you think might be taken in order to shift quadrant? If you're happy with the quadrant you are in, then reflect on how you stay there. What key factors keep you there?

So far, we have then a series of interesting comparisons: motivation versus productivity, and productivity versus manageability. Each comparison invites us to dig further into the causes, which means to identify what is really going on with a view to improving the situation; and also to increase our self-awareness,[13] as individuals and as teams.

Let's now consider the all-important issue of values and the contribution that a team makes to them. Figure 5.3 shows us a dynamic representation of what we were seeing in Figure 5.1.

If we look at Figure 5.3 we see almost a wheel which affects the ability of a top performing team to operate. The starting point for us is always the immediate, top of the wheel point of motivation. This is because motivation is energy and nothing moves without it. But different teams will have different foci, and one might well be higher purpose and the contribution to organisational values; notice the double arrows we put in where this occurs. This is because realising our values releases a tremendous amount of extra energy; it inspires us as well as motivates us, and this enables a redoubling or more of effort and energy.

However, the contribution to organisational values of a team, whilst a core contribution, is not so obvious a factor as productivity or manageability. For a start, it requires all employees in their respective teams to be aware of what the organisational values are, as well as living and working by

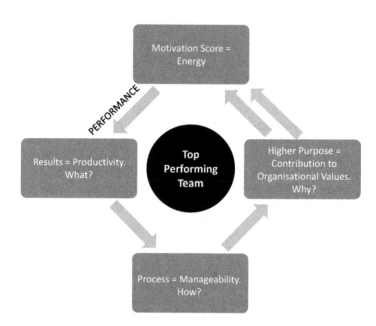

Figure 5.3 Motivation, Productivity, Manageability and Values

them; also, for senior executives to make this of first-order importance and to reward it accordingly.

Typically values need to be turned into behaviours. As a familiar example let us consider the core organisational value of honesty – being open and honest in all our dealings and maintaining the highest integrity at all times. As a behaviour this may become: all concerns are aired constructively with solutions offered and each person is as skilled in some way as another and is entitled to express their views without interruption. These two behaviours are 'honesty' manifested in behaviours towards employees; but equally, we may – indeed, should – have formulations of honest behaviours towards customers, suppliers, stakeholders and society generally. For how can it be said to be a true value if it is only selectively applied?

Of course, from the organisation values, team values arise, and these too must be treasured, repeated, re-enforced and rewarded. The longevity and ultimate success of the organisation depends probably as much on this key area as it does on the more obvious 'productivity'.

Further, values are motivational: at one end Defenders love them because they provide stability, and at the other the Searcher wants them because they create deep meaning in the work. Given this fact, we need to consider how motivational profiles may or may not support organisational or even team values. Do they work for them, or against them, or even reside in some neutral space?

Activity 5.5

Suppose the number one organisational value is Customer Focus, whereas a specific team's number one motivator is Spirit – autonomy. What issues may potentially arise from this situation?

Clearly here, there is the potential for the value and the motivator to be in conflict or to 'resist' the value rather than 're-inforce' it. This may be because the team resists or resents the constraints of serving the customer; it may not see either that how the customer is treated is just as important as what they receive; and the customer may also receive an inconsistent service or approach, as the Spirit tends to resist consistency or uniformity. We must insist of course that we are not stereotyping the Spirit motivator team as being incapable of Customer Focus; it's all going to depend on a number of factors, including other top motivators in the profile, the deployment of roles and individuals specifically, and leadership essentially. But the drift of Spirit is clear: it probably finds Customer Focus perhaps a little boring and inconsequential. On the other hand, if a value like Entrepreneurialism was number one for an organisation, then a Spirit team would ideally align with the value.

To take another, very different motivator: The Star. If a key organisational value were Recognition (in its widest sense), then the Star motivator might be thought to reinforces this value. However, this does not mean, 'value and motivator aligned, so job done'! Issues can arise even if there is alignment. One such 'issue' might be how there can be enough 'recognition' to go around to satisfy all? Another might be: is there a blind spot, or Achilles' Heel, or what we sometimes call in Maps a hygiene factor, in an over-concentration of one motivator?

With these thoughts in mind, then, let's look how we might tackle this. Figure 5.4 shows three columns in which we can consider how the values sit alongside the motivators.

The top operational values could include any number, but for the purposes of being manageable, we like to consider the top three: what absolutely are the top three values this organisation stands by and will not set aside under any circumstances? Here are the top three from a FTSE 250 company we worked with, three actually from a longer list; the values were expressed in fuller sentences, but to get to the essence we have abbreviated them to a key word and a couple of descriptors (see Figure 5.5).

These are extremely ambitious values, especially as they eschew 'content' (as in being profitable or having some sort of commercial or operational orientation) and focus on the process (as in the experience of working in the organisation and how that is going to feel). Needless to say, but we will, that the company has been highly successful over a 10-year period in precisely the content area of profitability and ROE.[14] But what are the organisation's top three motivators?

Organisational Values		
Top Operational Values	Relevant Motivator(s) from top 3	Re-inforce, Resist or Issue?

Figure 5.4 Organisational values and team top three motivators

VALUE : Teamwork	•Support and feedback.
Behaviour (example)	•Helping each other.

VALUE : Communication	•Listening and sharing.
Behaviour (example)	•Encouraging questions.

VALUE : Adventure	•Change positive.
Behaviour (example)	•Asking 'What can we do better or differently?'

Figure 5.5 Example of three top operational values for an organisation

Organisational Values		
Top Operational Values	Relevant Motivator(s) from top 3	Re-inforce, Resist or Issue?
1. Teamwork	1. Searcher	
2. Communication	2. Expert	
3. Adventure	3. Defender	
	Lowest : Friend	
	77%	

Figure 5.6 Top three values, top three motivators and the lowest!

If we look at Figure 5.6, how is this organisation of several hundred people doing – aside from its financial profitability (which I have already alluded to). The answer immediately is that it is doing very well from a motivational point of view: to score 77% for a whole organisation of its size is a tremendous result in itself; an average type of score for a company of this size might well be below 60%. But now we have to ask, what does this table mean?

Activity 5.6

The third column asks us to reflect on whether the values and the motivators are aligned. What do you think? Make some notes on any points or issues as you see them.

The key operational value of teamwork is well supported by both the Searcher motivator, seeking to leverage results through team synergies, so that a bigger difference can be made, and by the Defender motivator, which finds greater security and the possibility of better processes through team filters. The Expert motivator is somewhat neutral. Deployed as deep learning that can help others it is positive; but sometimes, particularly when coupled with the Defender motivator, the Expert can resist change and also hoard knowledge and expertise. Given the 77% score, it is highly likely here that the Expert motivator is reinforcing the values.

What about the communication value? Again we have the Searcher motivator prominently seeking to express what it is doing, and driving mission forward; but this time the Expert and Defender combination can be less helpful. Defender-type communications can become monochrome, or mono-channel, and repetitive so that they lose their edge. Combine this with too much information or 'geeky' expertise, and the required dynamism of communicating can be lost. It's as well, perhaps, that the specified behaviours tend towards very empowering types of activity such as 'encouraging suggestions'.

Almost finally, what about adventure? Well, certainly the Searcher is up for this – making a difference is always an adventure. But here again the Expert can get stuck in their expertise, and the Defender will not like change generally. Here is the area where the consultant or coach can add most value: is the organisation really able to sustain this value? And to answer that we need only look at the one behaviour we have specified from its list: how frequently are team members asking how things can be improved, or completely done differently? Is that part of the life of the team?

Finally, we need to comment on the lowest motivator, since it is a hygiene factor. As we have already established in Chapter 4, the Friend motivator is commonly lowest in many top performing teams, but it is dangerous if motivators stay that way. Here we have the same situation again: a top performing company with top performing teams within it; however, are the teams

Organisational Values			
Top Operational Values	Relevant Motivator(s) from top 3	Team: SMT	Re-inforce, Resist or Issue?
1. Teamwork	1. Searcher	1. Spirit	
2. Communication	2. Expert	2. Searcher	
3. Adventure	3. Defender	3. Expert	
	Lowest : Friend	Lowest : Friend	
	77%	90%	

Figure 5.7 Values, organisational motivators, team motivators

sustainable? It is true that the company has stayed at the top of its game for 10 years, but talking to HR one soon realises that there has been a lot of unnecessary churn[15] as key team members have moved on far too prematurely. What we said in Chapter 4, then, applies here too – see Figure 4.8.

But this little analysis is not the end. There is far more that can be done with this process.

What we now do is look at all or any teams within the organisation and see how they compare with the overall organisation. I have chosen the Senior Management Team itself in this example in Figure 5.7, since starting at the top is always a good idea. And here we see that there is not *much* difference from the organisational profile, but there is *a* difference and it is significant.

Activity 5.7

What is the significant difference and what might it mean? What else might be worth commenting on?

Clearly, a difference here is the change of the number one motivator: these company directors are actually motivated primarily by the Spirit motivator, and this also involves a polarity reinforcement with the Friend motivator, which is their least important motivator – as it is for the whole organisation. In other words, one might say that the senior team *intellectually* understands the importance of teams but are not going to be team players themselves! This, of course, will ultimately create cognitive dissonance as they fail to walk the talk of the core value of teamwork – and the requirement for support and feedback. Spirits find all that quite difficult to do, at least consistently.

The combination, too, of two Growth motivators in the top three suggests a much higher risk profile for the leaders, which is far more attuned to the Adventure value they espouse than the whole organisation. What we have, then, is potentially leadership from the top, but which is not wholly accepted or bought into by the teams – who are more cautious, more risk-averse, and so more likely to buy into teamwork and less likely to be adventurous.

Put another way, we can ask the question how far the organisation contributes to its values, and how much individual teams do; furthermore, we can then compare the contributions of each team alongside their motivational profiles and examine how far the motivational profile is responsible, or part responsible, for the situation the organisations and teams find themselves in.

In the case we have just studied the motivational differences were a profound and accurate indicator of what was going on: the senior management team were in fact in sync with contributing to the Adventure value, constantly driving new initiatives, but were far less attuned with the Teamwork value, even though that was considered a higher priority by most of their organisation. However, this took some explaining to clarify, since to persuade the senior people that they weren't fully contributing to organisational values seemed contradictory to them (see Figure 5.8). Weren't they the very people who set up the values? Yes, but setting them up and following them are two separate things.

Figure 5.8 shows us an actual, though selective, PMV assessment of four teams in the same organisation that we are considering; the motivation scores derive from Motivational Maps but the PMV scores are subjective estimates of the MD.[16]

Measuring Team PMV* Scores			
	Motivation %	Productivity / 10	Manageability / 10	Contribution to Org Values / 10
Customers	82	9	8	9
Admin	71	6	6	7
Managers	75	8	5	8
Senior Management	90	8	4	10
TOTAL				
AVERAGE				

Figure 5.8 Senior Team PMV assessments
PMV* scoring is for each team in each category out of 10, where 10 is outstanding and 1 is very poor.

Activity 5.8

What are the four most important points that these numbers reveal about the company and the teams, or indeed, the MD?

The first and most obvious point is what we have mentioned in terms of the Senior Management's self-perception: scoring his own senior team 10/10 for contribution to organisational values is a potential misreading of the situation. And we can see this is the case because the second point would be that, more honestly, the MD realises that his own team's manageability – that it to say, the team he leads – he scores only 4/10. This leads us to ask just how effective is the senior team when its own leader perceives its manageability at such a low score? Perhaps, to answer that question, we need to drill down further into the team map of this high performing team, which is Figure 5.11.[17] We will come to this in a moment.

But before that, however, we see how even at team level beliefs become reality. Admin clearly are viewed by the MD as the least effective team, which their own motivational scores bear witness to; surely, this is a commonplace: most Admin *departments* – as opposed to the word 'team' – are underrated in terms of their contribution to the whole organisation (see Chapter 7 for a striking exception to this), and so frequently remain less motivated than their peers. In this case, however, there is still at 71% a relatively strong motivation. In contrast, and unsurprisingly, though, given how crucial it is to the business, the customer service team is rated most highly. The managers are rated as productive, 8/10, but like their bosses seem not to be manageable, 5/10. Perhaps a case of like attracting like? Perhaps a case of that kind of maverick culture where individual results can be perceived as more important than the collective effort?

Finally, is there an actual correlation between motivational scores and the PMV overall? There would certainly seem to be between the motivation scores and the productivity scores, and also the motivation and contribution to organisational values; the motivation and manageability seem far less correlated, certainly at the managerial and senior managerial levels. And this, perhaps, gives us clues as to where some serious work needs to be done if – as we said – we want to build top performing teams for the long-term. If we set out the scores in a different way, setting the motivation scores alongside the average for the PMV scores and noting the difference, we get the following: see Figure 5.9.

The closer the scoring between the motivation and PMV scores, the more regular the pattern. So, for example, we see the motivation at 8 (80%) and the productivity at 8, which suggests an apt correlation; and we also see the values at 9, a good sign, but the manageability at 6, not so good. This gives us four possible scenarios (see Figure 5.10).

Figure 5.10 is a way of thinking about these data, but *not* in a prescriptive way. For as we examine the four possibilities, there are some suggestions

Measuring Team PMV* Scores			
	Motivation %	Productivity / 10	Manageability / 10	Contribution to Org Values / 10
Customers	82	9	8	9
Admin	71	6	6	7
Managers	75	8	5	8
Senior Management	90	8	4	10
TOTAL	318	31	23	34
AVERAGE	80	8	6	9

Figure 5.9 Reviewing PMV scoring

*We have here just taken an average from the team motivational numbers rather than a more exact computing from each individual's aggregated score, but as the overall score is 77% (or 8) this is accurate enough.

High Motivation Score

Low Motivation Score

Figure 5.10 Four quadrants of motivation and the PMV scores

as to what might be an issue in each of them. To be emphatic again, this is not prescriptive: for example, I have put leadership as a potential issue in the Low Motivation/Low PMV average score quadrant; but, of course, leadership could be issue in any of the other quadrants, including the High Motivation/High PMV quadrant. In this latter case, the leadership might be competent, but not outstanding, and so productivity and motivation could – with focus – improve even further.

So, returning to the question of leadership and our examination of the Senior Team itself and their contribution to the organisational values, it may seem that we have been rather harsh on them, especially considering their undoubted effectiveness and the fact that their organisation has – as its norm – many high performing teams. But we raised this issue because we felt that the scoring in Figure 5.8 didn't really tally. What does the Senior Team's own Team Motivational Map look like?

Obviously, with only three people in it, this is a very small and tight team. We can probably be pretty sure that the conclusions we have made so far are accurate as we look at this Map. The two conclusions are: first, that this team is not easy to manage, or manageable, and, second, that it is highly unlikely that it is fully contributing to the organisational values; and certainly not in a 10/10 way, as claimed!

Activity 5.9

Study Figure 5.11 and suggest why both these conclusions are likely to be correct.

Firstly, we note that all three members of the team have Spirit in their top three, which is why it is the dominant motivator; we also note that the Motivation Audit scores for the MD, HR, and FD's motivators are, respectively, 9, 9 and 10 (out of 10). In other words, they are experiencing massive levels of satisfaction which their job roles are allowing them. Their freedom and autonomy are not being constrained. In a bizarre way, it might be better for 'teamwork' if it were, but it is not. Therefore, we can see that they are not being managed by themselves (with an exception outlined in the next paragraph) and do not wish to be so. We can also see, in such a scenario, that

Name		Spirit	Searcher	Expert	Creator	Defender	Builder	Director	Star	Friend	Motivation Audit			
											%	1	2	3
Max	MD	25	29	32	23	24	17	8	11	11	82%	8	8	9
Kitty	HR	31	21	8	10	22	31	31	16	10	88%	9	8	9
Daryl	FD	27	32	24	29	16	13	17	10	12	100%	10	10	10
Total		83	82	64	62	62	61	56	37	33	90%			

Figure 5.11 The Senior Team's Motivational Map

they are highly unlikely to be contributing fully to the organisational team values.

Plus, we ought to comment on Kitty at HR. Whereas the MD and FD are very much aligned in their motivators, Kitty is not. The very strong – spike – motivators of Director and Builder, wanting control and competition, also militate against strong reinforcement at senior level of the team values. Interestingly, and as it proved (but positively), what might seem a source of conflict within the team, instead proved to be a necessary strength. The MD did not feel the need to be 'in charge' and Kitty's very strong Director and Builder (note, too, the Spirit is also equally scored at 31 – a real internal conflict in Kitty between her desire for control and freedom) meant that she wanted to provide management within the team, and pick up some of the more day to day issues, and was allowed to do so.

Charles Handy[18] talked about the 3i's of the modern age: information, from which in spotting patterns we generate intelligence; and from interrogating intelligence we can start deriving new ideas. Clearly, Maps are information driven, and from this we seek intelligence as to what is actually going on. Once that is established, we can formulate new ideas to stimulate further the success of the organisation or help them correct what they are doing in order to make improvements. Clearly, in this instance, given the success and seniority of the Senior Team, a simple training programme – implying a leadership deficiency on their part – is not going to cut it. Rather, the focus needs to be around what they all have in common: The Spirit motivator. In other words, a coaching programme that is specifically geared around what Spirits want.

What do they want? More effective time management – freeing up time – and tools and techniques that help them realise their own and the organisation's vision more comprehensively. And this is what we did. See the Resources section for seven Team Reward Strategies for the Spirit ideas that can potentially be utilised in this scenario. These (and the other motivational-type team Reward Strategies also listed there) can, of course, be used with any team we choose to inspect in this way.

We have covered a lot of new material in this chapter, but we are not yet done, for there is one more point that must be included here. Some of you may already have anticipated this: namely, Figure 5.8 is a highly revealing set of statistics to work from. But as with 360° appraisals, we can improve them by including more views in the analysis as Figure 5.12 shows.

We can go to the team itself and ask every member to rate itself according to the PMV criteria we have discussed, and with their Motivational Map score as the benchmark against which we are comparing progress. The important thing in doing this is to ensure all do it independently and

Team Member	Motivation	Productivity	Manageability	Contribution to organisation values
A				
B				
C				
D ...				
X				
TOTAL				
AVERAGE	Team Map Score	A+B+C+...X / X	A+B+C+...X / X	A+B+C+...X / X

Figure 5.12 Team PMV scores

without reference to each other. The same principles apply that we have discussed, but now the collective view adds real power and even deeper insights. Equally, Figure 5.12 can be adapted to be used by senior managers pooling their collective views about the teams under them. Either way, a treasure trove of insightful information and intelligence can be ascertained, and from this new ideas and ways forward be generated.

As we reach the end of this very long chapter – which is itself one of three – we are perhaps quite breathless, as it seems as if there is even more to say about The Remit! But now we must move on and cover another key characteristic of top performing teams: interdependence.

Notes

1 See these three articles on The Law of Three, parts 1, 2, and 3, James Sale, https://bit.ly/2vhlxxS, https://bit.ly/2I9cke1, https://bit.ly/386gHRD (2019).
2 The three forces – whatever their incarnation – may be summed up as follows: The Affirmer (the creator, the life-giver, the instigator); The Denier (the destroyer, the life-taker, the reactor); The Reconciler (the resolver, the bridge, the completer) – see The Law of Three Part 1, ibid. From the point of view of The Remit, What We Do might be considered the Affirmer, but what the customer wants or how they want to be treated might be the Denier. These might cancel

each other out, but the introduction of the Reconciler – our values in this case – might provide the bridge between satisfying both competing claims.

3 'At this, in a sense, deepest level of our value judgements, there is diversity, luckily, not consensus. The latter would demand regimentation of our intellectual and emotional life' – Arne Naess, *Life's Philosophy* (The University of Georgia Press, 1998).

4 See *Mapping Motivation for Coaching*, James Sale and Bevis Moynan (Routledge, 2018), Chapter 7, and *Mapping Motivation for Engagement*, James Sale and Steve Jones (Routledge, 2019), Chapter 6.

5 PMV criteria are how Productive (P) the team is, how easy it is to Manage (M) and how much does the team contribute to organisational Values (V)? That is, Productivity, Manageability and Values.

6 According to Geoff Petty, a leading educational researcher, 'Carl Rogers places self-assessment at the start and heart of the learning process. And the learning from experience cycle devised by Kolb places heavy emphasis on self-assessment'. https://bit.ly/3cd2jdj.

7 Fear is the great inhibitor of genuine performance; this is why W.E. Deming stated that driving out fear was a prerequisite to high performance and quality: Rafael Aguayo, *Dr. Deming: The Man Who Taught the Japanese about Quality* (Mercury Business Books, 1991).

8 There is, of course, always room for improvement in the future, but that does not mean that one cannot be a 10/10 in the present. It is a disabling and false modesty to believe that one cannot achieve the highest score, even though tomorrow the bar might be raised even higher. This conditioning is something that must be resisted and turned round: for more on tools to do so, see *Mapping Motivation for Coaching*, ibid., Chapters 5, 6, and 7.

9 See Stuart Watkins, 'The Productivity Puzzle: Is Britain Stuck in a Rut?', *MoneyWeek*, 29/11/2019.

10 For more on the distinction between people and things, see *Mapping Motivation for Leadership*, James Sale and Jane Thomas (Routledge, 2019), Chapter 8.

11 Philip Crosby, *Let's Talk Quality* (Penguin, 1992).

12 Which is paradoxical, of course, if we consider what we have said in Chapter 4 about the need for more awareness of Relationship motivators if we wish to have longevity. But a paradox is not a contradiction; it's an ambiguity we have to live with.

13 'There is one quality that trumps all, evident in virtually every great entrepreneur, manager, and leader. That quality is self-awareness. The best thing leaders can do to improve their effectiveness is to become more aware of what motivates them and their decision-making' – Anthony Tjan, Harvard Business Review, cited by Ian Morgan Cron and Suzanne Stabile, *The Road Back to You: An Enneagram Journey to Self-Discovery* (IVP Books, 2016).

14 ROE = Return on Equity, a classic measure at how effective an organisation has been in deploying its resources, especially its financial investment.

15 The churn was approximately 40% of staff per year before the advent of the mapping work, and this reduced to 25% after the programme completed its first phase. Operating profit increased by 40% too, but mapping staff was only one factor, in a wider programme, of this general and significant improvement.

16 So, this does not invalidate our earlier point about the main two sources of erroneous self-rating, since the MD in this case is not rating himself but the performance of his own team in very specific categories. In rating others, one can be wrong in one's assessment for a number of reasons, primarily cognitive

or psychological. In this instance, the component which is an actual self-rating would be that for his own Motivational Map; for this he scored 82%, which appeared highly accurate. Naturally, the self-ratings can be extended beyond one person, and this increases accuracy further: Figure 5.12.

17 For more information on this team and this team map, see *Mapping Motivation for Leadership*, ibid., Chapter 6.

18 Charles Handy, The London Business School, 2015, https://bit.ly/33atcur.

Chapter 6

Interdependency and motivation

In Figure 1.1 we learnt about the four characteristics of a team. We detoured to look at the vital question of Reward Strategies in Chapter 2, but then returned to the first of these characteristics, The Remit, in Chapters 3, 4 and 5. As it turned out, The Remit was a huge area to cover, and we considered three specific aspects of it from a motivational perspective: see Figure 6.1. But now our attention shifts to the second characteristic, Interdependency, and its relationship with motivation.

Teams require interdependency as life requires oxygen[1]; it seems simple, but it's not. There are so many factors working against interdependency.

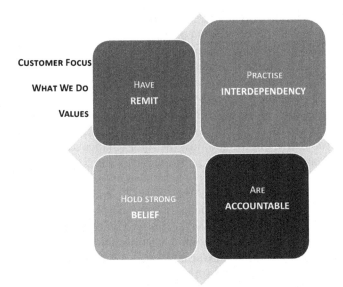

Figure 6.1 Practise Interdependency

Activity 6.1

What factors would you identify as working against interdependency within a team? If you had to rank them, what would be the top three factors preventing a top-performing team emerging?

There are, unsurprisingly, many factors that can derail a team. Some of these are external to the actual internal workings of the team: the recruitment process itself and then how new members are inducted (which may be externally structured), the reward structures and how appropriate and relevant they are, and perhaps crucially, at that point of interface between the external and internal, the leadership itself, which arguably is the single biggest factor and which if negative, undermines team cohesion. But internally, there are many other factors too: egoism, need-dependencies, personality conflicts, lack of knowledge and skills, and these factors can lead to very damaging behaviours. Behaviours such as restricting information, lying, breaking into sub-groups rather than solving problems together (sometimes called 'paring'), in-fighting with win–lose situations within the group, flight and withdrawal, noise – speaking to be heard rather than to contribute, suppressing emotion and demanding logic (when emotions may be part of the problem). So the list goes on.

However, if effective leadership has to be the number one factor working towards creating a high performing team, then perhaps the number two factor is going to be the recruitment process. This is something the leader is usually, and should be, involved in. People leave, people retire or die, new projects arise, and so we are in a constant state of flux: who is going to be in this team? Who, whether that be an internal or an external appointment? The balance of the team is crucial. Remember what we said in Chapter 1: *teams practise interdependency, not independency and not co-dependency! By this we signify that each person's gifts, abilities and talents are needed, are necessary, to achieve the remit or the objective. Not too many people, so there is redundancy and bloat; and not too few, so that there is under-capacity to deliver.* Not too many, not too few, just the right balance to achieve the goals.

And of course, alongside the recruitment go the Reward Strategies, for everyone who takes a job expects to be rewarded for it. So in a way, recruitment is like a tandem bike: we get the person in, and the rewards are on the second cyclist's seat, helping to pedal and driving the whole cycle forwards! You will notice, then, that my two choices for creating interdependency are either external or on the threshold. The 'threshold' here meaning the interface between internal and external factors – see Figure 6.2. What is the third most important factor? Rooting out egoism? Stamping out personality conflicts? Ensuring information flows?

These are all important in their own way, but our view is that we have not included one vital factor that in our experience is so important, and this is an internal one. It is of course motivation. Whereas everyone has heard of

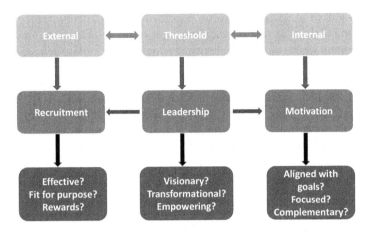

Figure 6.2 Recruitment, leadership and motivation

'personality conflicts', little thought has been given to 'motivational conflicts' and the damaging effects they have on teams. So our top three negative factors on team effectiveness range from the external to the internal factors, with that threshold point in the middle, leadership, being key. Figure 6.2 shows what this looks like.

The question of recruitment raises the further question of diversity in a team. Is this good or bad from a motivational perspective? Context is everything; there can be no easy or automatic answer. One contingency is always: what we are trying to achieve as a team? But as a general observation we would note that whilst everybody is claiming that 'diversity' is essential, what they mean by that is diversity of gender, race, religion, ability/disabilities, and other such categories; but what they clearly don't mean by it is diversity of opinion or thinking![2] Indeed, thinking 'differently' too often invokes a penalty or outright group rejection.[3] And just as thinking differently causes problems, so does motivational diversity; for, after all, diverse motivators drive us in unlike ways, which are often not acceptable if we feel (and feel strongly) differently!

And here's a really important point to consider: it's one thing having a different point of view, an alternative perspective on things, or what we might call a 'thought'. But however serious conflicts in thinking are, they are never so serious as when emotions are involved, and this is exactly what the underlying motivators are. Most of the time our thinking is not rational 'thinking', but rationalisations of our emotional desires. As the philosopher Spinoza observed,[4] 'In a state that is not marked by emotion, one makes no progress in anything that is essential to mankind'. Actually, what this means is that the really big conflicts in teams (and elsewhere) are highly likely the majority of the time to have some motivational root, because when our motivations are 'crossed' or blocked, as it were, it immediately affects our motivational, our feeling state, and this is much more provocative than some intellectual disagreement about ends and means to which we are not attached.

Thus, the top performing team will understand motivation and motivators as a routine matter of course, whether they use Motivational Maps or not. But the Maps enable a much more exact and accurate way of understanding what is going on motivationally. Before we come to them, though, let's consider recruitment again and what the high performance traits are that we are looking for in individuals we bring into a team.

Lou Adler,[5] one the world's leading recruitment experts, identified four traits or characteristics of individuals that we wish to recruit into any team.

Activity 6.2

What are the top four traits that you think you'd want in an individual recruited to a team that you were going to lead? And once you have identified them, which one do you consider the most important of all?

Figure 6.3 needs some unpicking to be clear about what we mean here. First, the most important trait of all is energy and energy-linked traits, such as drive, persistence and initiative. This should come as no surprise, since as we like to say, performance has three core elements: direction, skills/knowledge, and motivation. And if direction is the steering wheel of the car, skills/knowledge are the engine/chassis, then motivation is the fuel that enables the vehicle to travel at all.[6] Adler neatly suggests that high performance comes down to: talent × energy^2. Or, Figure 6.4.

Without getting into what 'talent' is – a highly ambiguous term[7] –the fact is that energy is motivation. The first thing we need to establish at the recruitment interview is whether the candidate is highly motivated or not. If the candidate is internal, we ought to know the answer to that question,

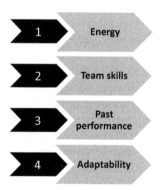

1 Energy

2 Team skills

3 Past performance

4 Adaptability

Figure 6.3 Four high-performance traits to recruit

Figure 6.4 Performance = Talent × Energy^2

but we can easily blindside ourselves by rationalisations that override the importance of motivation. Rationalisations such as: Anna knows her stuff, or Bert's been with us for 20 years and it's his turn, or even Sunak won't rock the boat, or everyone likes Frieda. As valid as any of these points may be, they don't alter the central fact: motivation – high energy – is the driver of the best sort of performance that produces results.

If the candidate is external, then we have the problem of working out whether the application, the CV, the references, and most importantly, the interview performance, really reflect the energy levels of the candidate. Again, according to Adler, interview performance does not measure or even reflect actual performance on the job; further, Adler reckons that whether you like or dislike someone can constitute some 70% of the hiring decision! In other words, we regularly hire using criteria that are not related to performance.

Thus, to find out whether somebody is really energised, we need to ask questions that delve into their past performance in a slightly indirect way.[8] We drill down, then, with repeated questions like: 'James, tell me about your current role and what has been your most significant success to date'. Clearly, the interviewee is being asked to show what they can do, but the interviewer(s) know that any significant achievement is underpinned by high energy levels, which is identical to high motivation levels.

So, if that's the case, then why not use Motivational Maps and go directly to the energy motivation question? This is not an either–or situation; rather, the Maps can complement and throw further and much deeper light on the candidate. Also, the candidate cannot second guess the meaning of the Motivational Map questions in the same way as they might the standard interview questions.

To get at this information, we need to tailor questions around the Map profile of the candidates; it is usually better if the interviewers do not discuss the actual Motivational Map of the candidate, but use it to consider how they respond to questions which we think we already know the answer to. This is a bit like the advice, often seen in cinematic court-room scenes, where the inexperienced lawyer is briefed by a more senior figure who instructs that one should never ask a question of a witness that one does not already know the answer to!

Motivator	Root Question	Check Question
Searcher	I see that making a difference is important to you. At the risk of sounding obvious, can you tell me why that is so?	Tell me how you've made a difference in your most recent role? What happened?
Spirit	I see that being able to make your own decisions is important to you. At the risk of sounding obvious, can you tell me why that is so?	Tell me about when you've been able to make your own decisions in your most recent role? What happened?
Creator	I see that being able to innovate is important to you. At the risk of sounding obvious, can you tell me why that is so?	Tell me about when you've been able to innovate in your most recent role? What happened?
Expert	I see that demonstrating expertise is important to you. At the risk of sounding obvious, can you tell me why that is so?	Tell me about when you've been able to demonstrate expertise in your current/most recent/last role/job? What happened?
Builder	I see that money is important to you. At the risk of sounding obvious, can you tell me why that is so?	Tell me about when you've been able to make more money in your most recent role? How did you do it?
Director	I see that actively managing is important to you. At the risk of sounding obvious, can you tell me why this is so?	Tell me about when you've been able to actively manage in your most recent role? What happened?
Star	I see that receiving recognition is important to you. At the risk of sounding obvious, can you tell me why this is so?	Tell me about when you've been receiving recognition in your most recent role? What happened?
Friend	I see that being part of a team is important to you. At the risk of sounding obvious, can you tell me why this is so?	Tell me about when you've been part of a team in your most recent role? What happened?
Defender	I see that security is important to you. At the risk of sounding obvious, can you tell me why this is so?	Tell me about when you've felt secure in your most recent role? What happened? How did that come about?

Figure 6.5a The Root and Check Questions for recruitment

From the Map perspective there are four major areas to explore based on the candidate's top motivator.[9] Two of these major areas are revealed in Figure 6.5a.

The Root Questions may be introduced by a phrase such as 'Looking through your application, I see that ...'. Notice that one doesn't say, 'I see from your Motivational Map that you are a Searcher and so that making a difference must be important to you' (and similarly for each motivator – adapt as appropriate). On the contrary (in as nonchalant and non-committal way as possible), we suggest that the application itself reveals that the candidate makes or wants to make a difference (and so on, for whatever is the number one motivator in the candidate's profile). And then we seek for them to answer WHY this is so. Essentially, we are investigating, as a detective might, how self-aware the candidate is. Generally speaking, high self-awareness is positive and enabling[10]: the candidate is likely to be more responsive to change.

But then, we have the Check Questions. These are not asking why a motivator is important to a candidate, but rather WHAT they have actually done or achieved. This corresponds in Adler's model to establishing past performance, since that is a likely indicator of future performance. As with the Root Questions, these too may be introduced by a short, non-committal phrase like, 'I see that making a difference is extremely important to you. Tell me ...'. And this question can be used iteratively: going back in time to roles prior to the one that candidate currently holds. Furthermore, the wording can also be modulated depending on which motivator (keep in mind, the top three tend to be the significant ones) we are focusing on. So, for example (and this is not prescriptive), we might say the top motivator is 'extremely important to you', but if we were dealing with their second highest motivator, we might say, 'very important to you', and the third motivator could just be 'important to you'. In this way we vary how much importance to the motivator we are attributing to the candidate.

Clearly, these are crucial questions, for they are establishing three key things.

Activity 6.3

What do you think the three key things are that Figure 6.5a establishes for the interviewers of a candidate?

First, whether or not we know what really motivates the candidate; second, whether or not the motivator leads to actual outcomes; and, third, whether or not the candidate is genuinely aligned with their own motivational profile. This alone may almost be sufficient to separate the high performing candidate from the less valuable applicant, the wheat from the chaff so to speak, but given the expense of making a wrong hire,[11] we may wish to dig even deeper. Therefore, still working with Motivational Maps, in Figures 6.5b (i), (ii), and (iii), we have developed two more powerful questions for each of the nine motivators that take our understanding of the candidate even further.

This deeper digging involves two kinds of questions. First, is the Creative question. Keep in mind that from the Root and Check Questions we have uncovered the WHY and the WHAT. Now we are effectively considering HOW the candidate operates in their motivational field – how creative they might be in the post that they are applying for. This is essential because as is said in selling financial products – 'past performance is not necessarily an indicator of future returns'. This is a get-out clause, for the truth is that past performance often is an indicator; a winner often wins,[12] and a formula that has been successful can often go on being successful. But if we think about Figure 6.3, what we are also driving at here is the 'Adaptability' principle[13]: being creative, flexible and resilient, being able how to solve problems for the organisation that one is about to join, is central. We are, therefore, in these Mapping Motivation style questions covering (from Figure 6.3): Energy, Past Performance and now Adaptability. Is the energy of the motivator really driving achievement? These three types of question – Root, Check and Creative – answer this.

But still we have not finished, because there is an aspect of human nature that we need to take into account: namely, what happens when things go wrong? How do we respond to that scenario? And here we come to the

Motivator	Creative Question	Block Question	Block Responses
Searcher	And tell me how you think you can make a difference in the post we have open?	Have you ever done work where you received very little or no feedback on how you were doing from anyone?	If NO – probe. Really? Never? Ask YOURSELF: Is this a credible answer? If YES – follow up: What did you do? How would you respond if you were working here and didn't receive the kind of feedback you initially envisaged?
Spirit	And tell me how you think you will be able to make your decisions in the post we have open? What are your expectations?	Have you ever been in a situation where you found yourself not able to control your own time and schedule?	If NO – probe. Really? Never? Ask YOURSELF: Is this a credible answer? If YES – follow up: What did you do? How would you respond if you found the work here more tightly managed/time inflexible than you initially envisaged?
Creator	And tell me how you think you will be able to innovate in the post we have open? What are your expectations?	Have you ever found work too routine and predictable for your taste?	If NO – probe. Really? Never? Ask YOURSELF: Is this a credible answer? If YES – follow up: What did you do? How would you respond if you found work here more routine and predictable than you initially envisaged?

Figure 6.5b (i) The Creative and Block Questions for recruitment: Growth Motivators

Motivator	Creative Question	Block Question	Block Responses
Expert	And tell me how you think you will be able to demonstrate expertise in the post we have open? What are your expectations?	Have you ever been in a role where there is too little development or learning necessary to accomplish it for your taste?	If NO – probe. Really? Never? Ask YOURSELF: Is this a credible answer? If YES – follow up: What did you do? How would you respond if you found work here more lacking in development and learning opportunities than you initially envisaged?
Builder	And tell me how you think you will be able to earn more in the post we have open? What are your expectations?	Have you ever been in a role where there has been too little opportunity to increase your income for your taste?	If NO – probe. Really? Never? Ask YOURSELF: Is this a credible answer? If YES – follow up: What did you do? How would you respond if you found working here did not provide you with the size of income that you initially envisaged?
Director	And tell me how you think you will be able to actively manage in the post we have open? What are your expectations?	Have you ever been in a role where there has been too little opportunity to actively manage for your taste?	If NO – probe. Really? Never? Ask YOURSELF: Is this a credible answer? If YES – follow up: What did you do? How would you respond if you found working here did not provide you with a sufficient scope to manage that you initially envisaged?

Figure 6.5b (ii) The Creative and Block Questions for recruitment: Achievement Motivators

subtlest parts of the interview questioning: The Block Question. That is, the question that explores what happens when our motivator(s) is blocked.

Activity 6.4

Reflect on your own top motivator, whichever one it happens to be. How do you feel when it is not being realised or met? And, even more so, how do you feel when it is not met over a prolonged period of time? What do you do? Think about this from your own work or role perspective or experience? Are you proactive, reactive, defensive, aggressive, passive, assertive or what? What changes occur in you when your motivator – or motivators – are not fulfilled?

I have spent some time getting you to think about this because it is vitally important. As the philosopher Arne Naess[14] put it: 'The road to freedom requires motivation through feeling …'. The freedom here is the freedom[15] to self-actualise, to be all we could be, or to realise our destiny. Actually, then, if the motivators are not met, we feel constrained, our sense of freedom is impaired. We are blocked!

Furthermore, it is only when there is constraint and pressure that we truly find out what somebody is like; for anybody can be likeable and popular, or a good person, when everything is going well. But what are they like when the tide turns against them? In a sense the Block Question is also establishing the character[16] of the candidate. So that the final Block Question is

Motivator	Creative Question	Block Question	Block Responses
Star	And tell me how you think you will be receiving recognition of the kind you want in the post we have open? What are your expectations?	Have you ever been in a role where there has been too little recognition for your taste?	If NO – probe. Really? Never? Ask OURSELF: Is this a credible answer? If YES – follow up: What did you do? How would you respond if you found working here did not provide you with the sufficient recognition that you initially envisaged?
Friend	And tell me how you think you will be part of a team in the post we have open? What are your expectations?	Have you ever been in a role where there has been too little teamwork or socialising for your taste?	If NO – probe. Really? Never? Ask YOURSELF: Is this a credible answer? If YES – follow up: What did you do? How would you respond if you found working here did not provide you with a sufficiently team-orientated environment that you initially envisaged?
Defender	And tell me how you think your need for security will be met in the post we have open? What are your expectations?	Have you ever been in a role where there has been too little security or predictability for your taste?	If NO – probe. Really? Never? Ask YOURSELF: Is this a credible answer? If YES – follow up: What did you do? How would you respond if you found working here did not provide you with a sufficient sense of security that you initially envisaged?

Figure 6.5b (iii) The Creative and Block Questions for recruitment: Relationship Motivators

about finding how the candidate reacts to the situation when the top motivator (and this can also be used for the second and third most important
motivators) is not being fulfilled. What did they do?

Here, however, there is an extra column which we call Block Responses.
Basically, the Block Question is deliberately set-up as a closed question;
in other words, it requires a Yes or No answer. Let's take one example to
see why. Take the Searcher motivator. Imagine this is the candidate's top
motivator.

Activity 6.5

Consider the Block Question for the Searcher: 'Have you ever done work
where you received very little or no feedback on how you were doing from
anyone?' There are two possible answers to this: either the candidate says,
'Yes, I have been in that situation' or they say, 'No, I haven't'. What are the
issues to consider in either case? If you prefer, use the example of your own
top motivator and substitute this question for the Searcher with the relevant
one for you from either Figure 6.5b (i), (ii) or (iii).

So the column Block Responses in the three Figures 6.5b gives a short-
hand summary of what we are looking for. Thus, if the answer is NO, this
means the candidate has never been in a job or role where (using the Searcher
example) there has been little or no feedback! Actually, that would be an astonishing feat, because one of the commonest complaints of all employees
everywhere is that they do not receive sufficient feedback.[17] But, it is not
impossible: the candidate could be very young and relatively new to the job
market, or could be a candidate who has only ever had one or two long-term
jobs that have been incredibly fulfilling. There is also a third alternative,
which is that the candidate has been in a role where the kind of feedback
we are talking about is perhaps less relevant; for example, they have been a
forester or ranger where they experience huge levels of individual autonomy
and are supposed to get 'lost' for months at a time in their role. That said,
all of this is relatively unlikely. Therefore, if the candidate says NO to this
question, we have to ask ourselves a different question: *Really*? Is this likely?
What is this candidate concealing? This is not to call them out directly, but
it is to explore what this might mean. For example, is this person delusional
about their role or their competence? Do they imagine they are doing such
a perfect job there is no need for feedback? A follow-on question to them,
then, might be: 'What do you think about feedback? How would you benefit
from this if you were to receive it?' Notice now how we have switched from
the closed question to more open ones; this is because we need to explore
the issue in detail.

Of course, if the answer – and much more likely response – is YES: I
have been in a situation(s) where I have received little or no feedback, then
this is where we – the interviewers – want to be, and what we want to find

out about; here is where we might learn about the candidate's character, persistence, growth and creativity. How did they respond to the absence of something their motivator indicates they crave?

The follow-up to YES is, then: What did they do (that is, realising that they weren't getting any meaningful feedback)? Again, looking at Activity 6.4, how did they respond (according to their own account of themselves)? Does it sound like they were proactive, reactive, defensive, aggressive, passive, assertive or what? And once they have answered that question, we can press them still further: How would they respond if they were working here and didn't receive the kind of feedback they initially envisaged and desired?

This follow-on question is very difficult to answer, especially if their previous answer is hardly convincing; at this point, the candidate will resort to clichés or generalities which show they have no real grasp of the issues, or internal resources, to be able to deal with difficult situations.

If we summarise where we are, we have reviewed interdependency as a core attribute of teams and found that recruiting the right people in the first place is of the first order of importance.[18] Furthermore, we have also discovered that using the Mapping Motivation system in the recruitment process can cover many bases: namely, establishing high levels of energy, compelling past performances, and demonstrating adaptability; three key criteria identified by Lou Adler. What we haven't dealt with is Point 2 of Figure 6.3: team skills.[19]

Clearly, these are very much at the heart of interdependency. In our previous books[20] we have covered many aspects of this, as our Preface to this book also noted. What we are looking for from the recruitment perspective is staff who can motivate, persuade, influence and negotiate with others, who can cooperate, collaborate and share an enthusiasm for The Remit, who can work together as a real team in other words. And this means, beneath the surface, high levels of self-esteem, self-confidence, emotional maturity, and the ability to take full responsibility for one's own actions. No blaming, no projecting, no denial; no passing the buck, then, no organisational politics, no playing the system. Getting the job done! Wow! That's a big ask.

The standard – and effective (if done well) – way of establishing these qualities without using the Motivational Maps is by drilling down on team related questions.

Activity 6.6

What are 'team related questions'? If you wished to establish whether a candidate was a team player or not, what sort of questions might you ask them? What would be the three most important ones?

The important thing here is to drill deep rather than accept superficial answers and simply move on to the next question in the list. There cannot be a definitive set of questions, but we like these three. Ask them, and ask

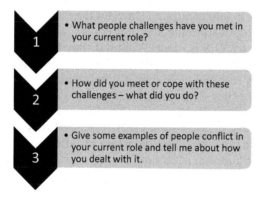

Figure 6.6 Three questions for team skills

for three examples in each case. Most people can drum up one answer, but it is going deeper than 'one' answer that reveals what is really going on. If necessary, go back several years and into previous roles or jobs. And feel free as you do this, to get the candidate to specify exactly what their role in the team is, who they answer to, and what results they have actually achieved.

As you ask these questions and study the answers to them, you will certainly find out about their team skills; and along the way their character, personality and possibly their fit into the culture of your organisation generally, and the team specifically. Quite a lot, then, may be revealed!

But here we come to where motivation and the Maps help us even more. For let us ask this question: can Motivational Maps identify high performing teams even without including the scoring? Clearly, if we include the scoring, then we know that high motivational scores *tend* to be correlated with high performing teams. This is also true of the individual – a point we will return to. But what about if we don't know the scores?

Activity 6.7

Why would we want to consider whether a team were high performing or not without looking at the scoring? Why not simply use the scoring as our guide?

The answer is that by checking via another Map methodology we increase the chances that we are going to get the correct answer. Truth is, just looking at the scores can make us lazy and too reliant on a simplistic equation: high motivation equals high performance – job done! But teams are made up of human beings, and human beings can be subtle and ambiguous, and not all is what it appears. Hence, the need to approach this issue in another way.

Motivation score = 77%

Figure 6.7 FTSE 250 company motivational rank order

The starting point of considering whether a team is functioning at a high level is the profile of the organisation itself. Here we are going to take a real life example from an anonymised FTSE 250 company.

Figure 6.7 shows the profile of a company employing several hundred people. It shows the rank order of the whole company's nine motivators. Whereas we are not going, initially, to know the motivational scores of the teams, it would be helpful to know how the organisation is doing motivationally: 77%. With so many hundred Maps aggregated, this represents a highly accurate benchmark score – accurate, that is, at that moment of time.

Activity 6.8

Figure 6.8 shows two teams from the same company. Both teams have the same function within the organisation, which is mainly customer service. They have approximately the same size too: team Yellow has 6 members and team Orange has 7. But the motivational scores have been removed. Their motivational scores do correlate with their respective performances; but without knowing them, which team – Yellow or Orange – do you think is high performing, and which less so? And what reasons do you have for this?

The first thing to study is how the teams compare with the company overall in terms of their top three motivational profile.

Inevitably, it must be the case that anything we say here is tentative. But the first thing to note is that Team Orange is more aligned with the Organisational profile than Team Yellow. This is particularly important regarding the top motivator, Searcher, which they share. It is particularly important because the top motivator is, by definition, the most important; but it is also significant because this motivator is very driven to make a difference

TEAM YELLOW

Member	Expert	Searcher	Spirit	Defender	Creator	Builder	Director	Friend	Star
A	22	22	21	23	19	19	16	21	17
B	18	20	19	20	19	19	22	20	23
C	28	18	26	22	21	15	22	11	17
D	21	18	32	16	27	21	31	5	9
E	30	35	10	25	25	15	18	13	9
F	26	27	25	22	16	26	5	25	8
Total	145	140	133	128	127	115	114	95	83

TEAM ORANGE

Member	Searcher	Defender	Director	Star	Expert	Creator	Spirit	Builder	Friend
G	28	24	17	18	21	17	17	19	19
H	33	27	13	24	17	17	16	13	20
I	25	20	25	25	15	10	30	30	0
J	24	28	20	25	27	20	16	17	3
K	26	18	27	22	27	16	15	15	14
L	35	21	21	14	23	21	11	13	21
M	29	19	32	18	7	27	22	17	9
Total	200	157	155	146	137	128	127	124	86

Figure 6.8 FTSE 250 Teams Yellow and Orange

for the customer – which both units are seeking to do. Since we know the organisation is highly motivated at 77%, the more correlated a team is with it, the more likely they are to be high performing. Why? Because they are aligned – fit – motivationally; their energies are moving in the direction of the same stream.

	1st	2nd	3rd	Lowest	
Organisation	Searcher	Expert	Defender	Friend	
Team Yellow	Expert	Searcher	Spirit	Star	
Team Orange	Searcher	Defender	Director	Friend	

Figure 6.9 Comparison: organisation with Teams Yellow and Orange

A secondary point would be that whereas the Organisation and Team Orange both share Friend as their lowest motivator (again in sync, as it were), Team Yellow has Star. This might indicate that there is a lack of recognition either for the team or certain members within it.

Finally, although doubtless there is more to be mined from the details, there is the fact that Team Yellow has the Spirit in its top three, whereas Team Orange has the Director entering the fray: Spirit and Director are conflicting motivators, sending one in entirely different directions. But given how low Spirit is organisationally (ranked sixth – Figure 6.7), this kind of autonomy and its functioning doesn't seem desirable, or what the organisation is really about. Indeed, the combination of the Searcher/Defender suggests a very process driven approach to customer service, and the Spirit motivator is not that.

And based on these musings, we find we would be right if we look at the actual scoring of the team maps.

Activity 6.9

Consider Figures 6.8 and 6.10 together. From it you will be able to see how each individual feels about their top three motivators. For example, team member A is 80% motivated, and he scores his top three motivators as follows: Defender (7/10), Searcher (10/10) and Expert (9/10); and so for the rest. When you have studied this, give three reasons, based on the numbers, why Team Orange is high performing and Team Yellow is not.

First, and mostly obviously, the team scores themselves indicate a fundamental difference in energy: Team Yellow on 59% is in the Risk Zone, whereas Team Orange at 85% is in the Optimal Zone. This is highly significant on an individual level, but is even more so when compounded at team level. Team Orange is thriving energetically and this will certainly be reflected in its results.

Second, the variation in scores, or the range between the highest and lowest, is far more marked in Team Yellow (88–10, or a range of 78 points) than in Team Orange (100–66, or a range of 34). This suggests far greater

Motivation Audit			
%	1	2	3
80%	7	10	9
26%	1	9	1
86%	10	5	8
88%	8	10	10
10%	1	1	1
62%	6	8	5
59%	Team Yellow		

Motivation Audit			
%	1	2	3
86%	9	7	9
66%	8	6	3
82%	10	1	10
100%	10	10	10
68%	7	7	6
96%	10	9	9
100%	10	10	10
85%	Team Orange		

Figure 6.10 Map scoring for Team Yellow and Team Orange

stability and consistency in approach, and this in turn suggests better management.

Finally, we can look at the specific individual scores. We note that the lowest motivated person in Team Orange is person H, who is only 66% motivated, whereas in Team Yellow we have two people, B and E, who are, respectively, 26% and 10% motivated; very low scores indeed. Without these two characters the average would be approximately 75% as the team score; but that's still well below Team Orange's 85%. However, a subtler overview might consider the actual individual audit scores.

A score of 6/10 we regard as average. In Team Orange there are only two scores below 6/10: H scores 3/10 for their third motivator (Star) and I scores 1/10 for their second motivator (Builder). Actually, I's overall scoring pattern requires comment, and we will return to this in a moment. But first, if we look at Team Yellow, we have B, who has scored their first and third motivators 1/10 (Star, Friend), C who has scored their second motivator 5/10 (Spirit), E who has scored all three motivators 1/10 (Searcher, Expert, Defender), and F, who has scored their third motivator 5/10 (Builder).

If we therefore now return to Activity 6.9, we see that whereas in Team Orange we only have two team members with specifically low motivator fulfilment, in Team Yellow we have four; and the low scoring is far wider ranging and more acute.

But in doing this analysis, we get extra information too: there are only two motivators that recur as problematic across the two teams: the Star and the Builder. Are people within teams getting enough recognition? And how does remuneration compare across the industry sector? This is an important point that might help Team Orange sustain its already high level of motivation and performance, and address some festering issues within Team Yellow which are holding it back.

Finally, there is one extra point to address: the profile of team member I. Whilst the motivational score overall is high, 82%, the numbers that make it up are a cause for concern. Indeed, if this person were a candidate at recruitment, then the fact of being 82% motivated might not be taken at its face value. The reason for this is the numbers themselves, see Figure 6.11.

Activity 6.10

Look at the numbers for I's profile. What strikes you as 'odd' about them?

One can never emphasise enough that Motivational Map readings should always be tentative; we are dealing with an inherently ambiguous property, and because motivations can change almost overnight in some circumstances, one must not make definitive comments. But what the motivational profile does is point to possible explanations or areas of interest that might affect how an individual or a team might perform in the long run.

What is 'odd' in Figure 6.11 is two-fold. First, that the nine motivator scores are all multiples of 5. Usually, when this occurs[21] we have potentially a false or misleading result. And secondly, that the Map will certainly be an extreme one: that is, the range of scores will be extremely wide.[22] Given that the average range from top to bottom score is about 8 points, here we have a range of 30 (0–30).

We recommend that anyone doing the Map does not agonise for too long by trying to second guess their own answers, but that is quite different from dashing down extreme and polarised scores: every answer must be 5–0 or

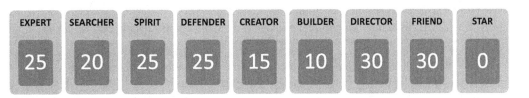

Figure 6.11 Motivation numbers for team member I

0–5 with no shades of grey in between. So, how likely is this to be an accurate representation of one's real motivators? It's possible, because there are really extreme people out there, but it is not likely, and so in typical Motivational Maps fashion, and especially at the interview stage, this needs examining carefully.

If, then, we want a top performing team, here is an issue for Team Orange: it is high performing, but the individual, I, may not be fully aligned with what is going on, despite an apparently high score of 82%. In Team Yellow we have the obvious fact that team members, B (26%) and E (10%), need attention, for their scores are dragging down the whole team. But sometimes the high scores too need attention. The percentage scores are important, but must not be considered in isolation.

Finally, keep in mind that the motivational profile may indicate the existence and practise of team skills, although it does not specify what they are or may be. In other words, high levels of motivation frequently presuppose the acquisition of whatever is needed to deliver the outcomes because such energy drives The Remit. Simply training people on 'team skills' is counterproductive if they are not motivated in the first place. In a top performing team motivation precedes the acquisition of skills.

We have, therefore, now looked at some key motivational aspects of interdependency and how teams cohere through motivational recruitment and also via the motivational profiles themselves. Our next chapter considers Belief and Top Performing Teams.

Notes

1 And additionally, as the Motivational Mapper, Paul Kinvig, likes to say: 'Motivation is like air; it's terminal when it's not there'.
2 A scathing comment reflecting on this issue came from Ben Shapiro: '"Diversity is our strength" is Orwellian claptrap coming from people who can't handle a memo that says that men and women are different' – Ben Shapiro, editor Daily Wire, quoted in the *MoneyWeek*, 12/8/2017. Shapiro was indignant that a Google engineer had been sacked from expressing what he saw as a non-controversial point. The sacked engineer posted an internal memo called Google's Ideological Echo Chamber. The text and Google's response can be found at https://bit. ly/39hNzHq.
3 Hence the phenomena of 'groupthink', which we have commented on before in our previous books; the subtle pressure that ultimately leads everyone to agree and think the same. See *Mapping Motivation for Engagement*, James Sale and Steve Jones (Routledge, 2019), Chapter 4. Also, Group-think, a concept outlined by Irving Janis, *Victims of Groupthink; a Psychological Study of Foreign-policy Decisions and Fiascos* (Houghton Mifflin, 1972).
4 Cited in Arne Naess, *Life's Philosophy* (The University of Georgia Press, 1998). Naess himself percipiently notes that 'Reason loses its function where there is no motivation, and motivation is absent where there are not feelings either for or against'. Donald Calne expressed this another way: 'The essential difference between emotion and reason is that emotion leads to action while reason leads to conclusions' – see https://bit.ly/2r019eS. It should be clear from this, therefore,

that motivational conflicts – because they are inherently energised – are a major source of conflict within organisations, teams and between people.

5 Lou Adler, *Hire with Your Head: A Rational Way to Make a Gut Reaction* (Wiley, 1998).

6 This formula for performance runs through all our work, but especially see: *Mapping Motivation*, ibid., *Mapping Motivation for Coaching*, James Sale and Bevis Moynan (Routledge, 2018), and *Mapping Motivation for Engagement*, ibid., Chapter 1, for an advanced formula or 'take' on these ideas.

7 The seminal book on this topic, *The War for Talent*, Ed Michaels, Helen Handfield-Jones, and Beth Axelrod (Harvard Business Press, 2001), perhaps unsurprisingly fails to define 'talent', saying: 'A certain part of talent elude description: you simply know it when you see it... We can say, however, that managerial talent is some combination of a sharp strategic mind, leadership ability, emotional maturity, communications skills, the ability to attract and inspire other talented people, entrepreneurial instincts, functional skills, and the ability to deliver results'.

8 Asking any candidate: Do you have high levels of energy/motivation in your work? Is, of course, only going to elicit a broad grin and the answer, Yes!

9 In fact, this is a simplification for the sake of space: the second and third ranking motivators can also be explored in this way; and it is also prudent to investigate the lowest motivator and what this might mean for the individual's performance in a given role, and for the team cohesion.

10 One scarcely need prove this point, since there is so much evidence around it, and it also seems like common sense, given a moment's reflection on one's own experiences. Psychiatrists and psychotherapists Jeremy and Roz Holmes in their book *The Good Mood Guide* (Orion, 1996), express it powerfully thus: 'Self-observation is in itself transformative, in an extraordinary way'.

11 According to BreezyHR, the real cost of a bad hire is always going to be a little different depending on your business. But citing data from the US Dept of Labor, The Undercover Recruiter and CareerBuilder, they give three cost scenarios: 1. The cost of a bad hire can reach up to 30% of the employee's first-year earnings; 2. Bad hires cost $240,000 in expenses related to hiring, compensation and retention; 3. 74% of companies who admit they've hired the wrong person for a position lost an average of $14,900 for each bad hire. See https://bit.ly/3aMM3Pd.

12 Although, of course, we acknowledge that expression made common in popular music: the 'one-hit' wonder!

13 This requirement for 'adaptability' has become a virtual movement in the last decade or so. In 2019 LinkedIn ranked it the fourth most desired soft skill companies want (https://bit.ly/2WZyKXr). In 2018 Accenture said that 'Adaptability to become top skill in 10 years' (https://accntu.re/3dJKEeb). And the Institute for the Future in 2018 claimed that 'Adaptability... essential skill for the future'. See: *AI Forces Shaping Work & Learning in 2030*, Report on Expert Convenings for a New Work + Learn Future, October 2018.

14 Arne Naess, ibid.

15 And it is not the Spirit motivator per se; to take one example, the Defender motivator itself will feel 'free' or freer when the motivator of security is met. This seems a contradiction almost, but it is not: a motivator we want, even if it seems to constrain us, enables us to feel freer – certainly of the anxiety caused by not having it met.

16 Thomas Merton wrote, 'Souls are like athletes that need opponents worthy of them, if they are to be tried and extended and pushed to the full use of their powers', *The Seven Storey Mountain* (Harcourt, 1998).

17 A recent article in *Forbes* magazine suggested that 65% of employees want more feedback! That's a large number. Victor Lipman, '65% Of Employees Want More Feedback (So Why Don't They Get It?)', 8 August 2016, https://bit.ly/2JDfWW1

18 Jim Collins, *From Good to Great* (Random House Business Books, 2001) makes the point that it is far easier to recruit the right people on the bus before you start the journey than to discover once you've started that you have the wrong people.

19 For more on team skills and specifically the Five Elements model of team skills, see *Mapping Motivation for Leadership*, James Sale and Jane Thomas (Routledge, 2019), Chapter 4. Also, see Chapter 6 of *Mapping Motivation for Engagement*, ibid., for four specific team skills of the Engaging Manager: cognitive/perceptual, interpersonal, presentational, and motivational.

20 Specifically, *Mapping Motivation*, ibid., Chapter 6 looked at motivation and teams; *Mapping Motivation for Engagement*, ibid., Chapter 6, considered the role of the engaging manager for the team; and *Mapping Motivation for Leadership*, ibid., Chapter 6, explored how leaders build teams and how to create team agreements.

21 One notable exception to this rule is the extremely rare (three occasions in over 70,000 Maps) when the nine motivators are all equally scored: all 20/40. This is a multiple of 5, but the comments in the text do not apply to this situation. The score seems to be accurate, and the individual is lacking in decisive motivators; the role of the coach or manager here is to help them set effective targets or goals that they can get behind, given their generally weak drivers. See Figure 7.7 for a real example.

22 Alongside the wide motivational scores, the satisfaction scores too are extreme: 10–1–10, suggesting he is totally satisfied with some motivators and totally unsatisfied with others. This necessitates looking at this individual's complete 22 numbers: do they all exhibit this tendency? And yes, they do: his satisfaction scores in the rank order of his motivators are: 10, 1, 10, which we already know, and then 10, 5, 5, 10, 5 and 10. The 'odd', not multiple of 5, is the second motivator, but overall this doesn't obviate the impression that this person is seeking to make an impact or statement in doing the Map. As we said before, this needs careful examination.

Chapter 7

Belief and top performing teams

We come now to the third element of a top performing team: Figure 7.1 emphasises the need for team members to hold strong Belief(s) if the team is really going to function at a high level. In Figure 1.2 we indicated that mere groups of people working together had no specific beliefs or even false beliefs and furthermore were invariably infected with a certain kind of negativity.[1] This negativity may not even be any individual's fault; they may simply have been recruited and joined a negative group of people. But this negativity can hold them, too, in its grasp, especially after resistance to it is exhausted; one comes to believe nothing can or will change and this is just the way things are.

But what kind of beliefs are we talking about and why are these so important?

Figure 7.1 Holding strong Belief

Activity 7.1

Why are beliefs so important? And, recalling material in Chapter 1, which beliefs specifically are critical for a high performing team?

Beliefs are critically important. Motivation itself[2] depends upon beliefs and expectations for its existence; in other words, beliefs help generate motivation. But more than just motivation depends on our belief systems. At the philosophical level William James[3] expressed it this way: 'Belief creates the actual fact'. At the parapsychological level,[4] 'Few laymen realize what parapsychologists have known for years – that, strangely enough, belief and expectancy themselves actually create phenomena, rather than the other way round'. And at the personal development and business level,[5] 'People become really quite remarkable when they start thinking that they can do things. When they believe in themselves, they have the first secret of success'. There is a wealth of evidence, both theoretical and experiential, that our beliefs affect reality and the outcomes of our lives.[6]

Specifically, however, when it comes to top performing teams there is one belief in particular that it is crucial to maintain, and also to *really* believe. We emphasise the word *really* here because anyone can say they believe it, and anyone can intellectually believe it; but sadly intellectually 'believing' it, is not believing it! This is rather like the work we covered in Chapter 6 on recruitment: everyone comes to an interview claiming to be the right candidate, claiming a track record of achievement, claiming they are the perfect fit for the job, and in one sense they often *believe* it. But the purpose of the interview is to expose these beliefs for what they are[7]: to find where the fit doesn't fit, to discover where the achievement record falls short, and why the candidate is indeed not the right candidate. At least, to do these things until the right candidate actually is found.

With this in mind, then, we have to realise that believing in the superior efficacy[8] of team work is not an option, or a thought; what we are alluding to is a belief that has an emotional component that drives us – like motivation itself – to act. If we really believe something, then we act accordingly. And this becomes something similar to what John Stuart Mill[9] expressed well over a century ago: 'One person with a belief is equal to a force of ninety-nine who have only interests'. Imagine what a whole team might be, then!

The most obvious way of seeing, or better, proving this is by results. It's all very well seeing sporting teams win glory and then attributing it to teamwork, or some company in a journal gaining market share and likewise attributing it to their great teams. But results take time, and however well sports teams and other business teams do, we personally may not have 'felt' this for ourselves. They remain examples, but we may not be motivated to want to emulate them. As Dr Alan Watkins[10] said, 'We still need the motivation to change and the optimistic belief that change is actually possible'. We may need a shortcut to help our people believe in teamwork; and one of the most powerful ways in which we can get buy-in from a team to this belief is by simulation. A simulation replicates what happens in the real world but does so in a safe environment where the risks of permanent damage – for example, to motivation and performance – are minimal.

There are various simulations that may do this but our favourite that has been in the public domain[11] since the early 1970s is the NASA[12] Moon exercise. This is a way of 'proving' teams outperform individuals, and it is very compelling. One aspect of being a top performing team is through making the right decisions. Therefore, what if we can, in an unknown situation that 'sort of' replicates what organisations face all the time,[13] get individuals to make decisions and then compare these individual decisions with a collective team decision?

Here's how it works.

Activity 7.2

Instructions: You are part of a space crew originally scheduled to rendezvous with a mother ship on the lighted surface of the moon. Due to mechanical difficulties, however, your ship was forced to land at a spot some 200 miles from the rendezvous point. During re-entry and landing, much of the equipment aboard was damaged and, since survival depends on reaching the mother ship, the most critical items available must be chosen for the 200-mile trip. In Figure 7.2 are listed the 15 items left intact and undamaged after landing. Your task is to rank order them in terms of their importance in allowing your crew to reach the rendezvous point. Place the number 1 by (in the blank left hand column) the most important item, the number 2 by the second most important, and so on through to number 15, the least important. Try this now for yourself. And, if you are in a group or team, including your own friends or family members who may be to hand, then ask them to do it, and once they have, do it collectively as if you were a team producing one rank order between you.

When you have done this, you will be keen to know how accurate your rank order is compared with NASA's rank order. It is important to stress at this point that the NASA rank order must be taken as 'gospel', as it were; there can be no arguing with their rank order, even though this was created over 50 years ago and since then new information has obviously emerged. Having conducted this exercise dozens of times, every now and then some 'expert' in the team pops up and knows better than NASA! The rules of the game are that this is not allowed.

But before seeing the actual answer, or anybody else's – for remember, we may have here a team of up to a dozen people all independently rank ordering the 15 items – we now ask the team to do it collectively; that is, to produce a team rank order, so that we can compare this with the individual answers. Once that is done, we can begin the analysis as per Figure 7.3.

NAME
Box of matches
Food concentrate
50 feet of nylon rope
Parachute silk
Portable heating unit
Two .45 calibre pistols
One case of dehydrated milk
Two 100 lb tanks of oxygen
Stellar map (of the moon's constellation)
Life raft
Magnetic compass
5 gallons of water
Signal flares
First aid kit containing injection needles
Solar-powered FM receiver-transmitter

Figure 7.2 NASA rank order decision form

Item	Brief Reason	NASA answer	Own answer	Difference 1 = score	Team answer	Difference 2 = score
Box of matches	No oxygen	15				
Food concentrate	Can live quite a while without food	4				
50 feet of nylon rope	For travel over rough terrain	6				
Parachute silk	Carrying	8				
Portable heating unit	Lighted side of moon hot	13				
Two .45 calibre pistols	Some use for propulsion	11				
One case of dehydrated milk	Needs water to work	12				
Two 100 lb tanks of oxygen	No air on moon	1				
Stellar map (of the moon's constellation)	Needed for navigation	3				
Life raft	Some value for shelter or carrying	9				
Magnetic compass	Moon's magnetic field is different from earth's	14				
5 gallons of water	You can't live long without this	2				
Signal flares	Distress call when line of sight possible	10				
First aid kit containing injection needles	First aid kit might be needed but needles are useless	7				
Solar-powered FM receiver-transmitter	Communication	5				

Figure 7.3 Analysis of NASA rank ordering for individuals and team
A Own Sum of Difference1 = _____ (total the scores in the Difference1 column)
B Team Sum of Difference2 = _____ (total the scores in the Difference2 column)

To help understand how to do this and what the scores mean,[14] consider the following: suppose in row two, Box of Matches, we have, for example, our Own answer as 12. Then, the Difference1 Score from NASA's correct answer is $15-12 = 3$. And suppose the Team answer is 14, the Difference2 Score is $15-14 = 1$. Clearly, the lower the sum of difference scores, the better the individual or team performance because the nearer it is to the correct NASA score. If the individual or team answered 15 then the difference would be $15-15 = 0$. Ideally, then, an individual or a team would score 0 for each of the 15 items, and their total deviance from NASA's answers would be 0 too![15]

Hence, in this way, each individual in the team can see two things: one, how their own personal result compared with NASA's correct rank order. They cannot beat NASA but if their score is 0, they have correctly got all 15 items in the right order. Second, they can see whether the team score is better than their own. We show this beneath Figure 7.3 as A. own sum of difference versus B. team sum of difference. Typically, in an average team (maybe one recently formed for a specific project) the team score can be around 30, whereas individual scores may be more like 60! This means the decision making is twice as good if the team makes it, as opposed to individuals in the group making it. Sometimes team decisions can be three times better than the group of individuals' decisions. If we could get real team decisions, what might that do for your business or organisation?

Activity 7.3

We cannot answer what it would mean for you, but imagine it: if your team(s) could make decisions that were at least twice as good as the individual decisions made within the team, what would that do for your business or organisation? Where would its effects most be felt: in sales, marketing, customer service, finance, operations? Where?

Frequently in doing this NASA simulation, everybody scores worse than the team score; and occasionally one person outperforms the team score, but everyone else fails to. The point is, in doing this, the conviction that a team outperforms an individual, is astonishing: many delegates are frankly amazed by the result, because they have been so reliant on their own skill, knowledge, sense of prowess. To find that the team performs better than they can – despite having subscribed to a team mantra in an intellectual way – comes as a complete shock to their system; and, also a profound wake-up call. The team leader can use this new awareness immediately as the team faces their next challenge or project. Also, if there is one person who outperforms the team, then who is this person? Are they generally taken seriously? Does it come as a surprise as to who it is? These questions all bear thinking about.

But two words of warning. As with reality generally, and people specifically, there is always the possibility that one can get a 'wrong' or reverse result; though even this can prove useful. As mentioned before, having conducted dozens of these NASA team exercise, rarely – but predictably – one comes across a result where the individuals outperform the team, and sometimes massively so. On investigation, two reasons keep popping up time and again, and one needs to be aware of these.

First, a possible reason why the 'wrong' result occurs and the individuals outperform the team is what I have come to call 'expert deference'. To give a clear example from my own experience: I once did the exercise with a team of Heads of Faculty in a large secondary school, and this included one individual who was head of physics. Therefore, it was assumed – and he assumed very dogmatically – that he knew all about lunar conditions and science. So naturally, the heads of English, history, geography et al. all deferred to his opinion. Thus, the team scoring became almost identical to his personal scoring, and that was plain wrong. He – no surprise – would not accept the NASA result, which said all that needed to be said about team-playing. And it was also noticeable how his 'authority' shut down all real discussion, because – he *knew*.

If that is bad enough, a worse scenario sometimes ensues. But this time instead of the expert deference, we have the 'boss deference'. Here is where exactly the same process happens as with the self-appointed 'expert', only instead of the expert we have the boss, or manager, or team leader, and the culture is such that everyone defers to their opinion. There is no healthy exchange of views. As soon as the boss expresses an opinion, the 'yes-men' and 'yes-women' agree that that makes sense. What makes this the 'worst' scenario is the fact that they are the boss, and if they have created that culture, they may well like it and want it to continue. There will be, therefore, a lip-service adherence to team-building[16] (of which the NASA simulation may be a manifestation), but in reality there may well be a 'no-change here, please' situation. This, clearly, is a delicate issue that will call forth all the powers and skills of the consultant involved to resolve.[17]

But however that may be, we should have established through the simulation that teams outperform individuals, and that belief, if activated within each individual, will produce fruit. Like the motivators themselves, it becomes a source of energy and stimulus to greater levels of performance. And once having done the simulation, the leader can constantly remind them of it, and spur them on to use team working even more effectively.[18]

This, then, is one foundational building block of building belief in the team, as opposed to subscribing to pure self-reliance, and every person in it for themselves. What else helps develop strong belief in the team? I often quote Virgil, 'Success nourished them; they seemed to be able, and so they were able'.[19] In that brief expression we have the essence for ongoing belief: 'success nourished them …'. In other words, our belief in the power of what we are doing is strengthened every time we get results; for that is what success is – it's getting results.

Goal-setting, targets, milestones, celebrating achievements along the way, these ideas are all well-known, well-trodden, and we approve of them. Our book, *Mapping Motivation for Leadership*,[20] deals with several of these ideas in some detail. Effectively, then, teams grow in belief the more success they achieve, or results they produce that prove that what they are doing is working. Just as we have feedback from leaders, and from team members (each other) which might be termed internal feedback, so results are what might be termed the external feedback from the environment.

We acknowledge, therefore, the importance of this, but pass over it here because our primary concern is how motivation might strengthen belief in the team. So, what can we do motivationally to improve belief in teams? The answer in one sense is surprisingly simple, for the issue of belief in teams is analogous to the issue of belief in motivation! From the start of this whole series of Mapping Motivation books we have made the point that motivation is a feature of organisational life, but a feature that is not perceived as a benefit; rather, organisations seek to measure performance, productivity and profit – the big three 'Ps'. It is easy in this scenario to overlook the fact that motivation drives performance – which drives productivity – which leads to profits (given the right strategy). Motivation is, therefore, the invisible component of success. What if, instead of bringing in motivational speakers or having Ra-Ra 'motivation' days, we seriously started tracking motivation in teams and using this as a basis for developmental work?

In Chapter 8 we will look at the motivational accountability of teams within an organisation; but now let's consider how the team becomes motivationally accountable to itself and thereby strengthens its belief in itself. The way we do this is by team tracking.

Let's consider the case of a real professional services company, which we'll call ABS Ltd. ABS caters to the Building sector of the economy. It has approximately 50 employees, although this varies over time (and depending on economic conditions), and these staff make up about 10 teams, though this again varies. Some teams are technical, some commercial, and there is of course a senior team and what I am going to call an Admin team. I say 'going to call' as the team does more than just 'admin' – because the company runs a tight ship, the team was initially run by the Finance Director (FD) and its brief included HR functions! Anyone familiar with SME businesses will recognise this scenario! It's certainly not ideal because FDs tend not to be ideal HR experts; and it's also not ideal including specific HR functions amongst all the administrative work, particularly hiring new staff.

But this is the team I'd like to focus on because it's self-belief over a long period of time was, in my view, quite astonishing, and proved a mainstay for the company. And yet, as so often with 'heroes/heroines', they went largely neglected: they weren't in sales and they didn't possess the technical skills which the company traded on. Admin teams, expressed another way, are a cost to the business; and they tend – everywhere – to be low down in the pecking order. Certainly, they are not paid as well as other more 'important' departments or teams. It's rather like the fact that the brain does the thinking, the muscles do the lifting, so we rarely think about the blood which circulates around all parts of the body, and – in one important sense – like the skin that keeps it together or keeps it functioning.

Activity 7.4

Take a look at Figure 7.4. Here we see a comparison of the motivational scores for ABS as an organisation with those of its Admin team for four, though not consecutive, years: years 1 and 2, and then a 4-year gap after which years 6 and 7 have completed the Maps. We'll talk about this shortly, but for now – given that we are focusing on belief – what might we say about these scores and how they compare?

The Motivational Maps are a self-perception inventory; this means that an individual measures themselves against themselves and not against each other or some external standard. Measuring ourselves against each other can produce counter-productive animosity between individuals and between teams; but the reality is, we always want to know how other people are doing. It provides a benchmark for how we are doing, and it can spur us on. Furthermore, in seeing that we are doing better than others, we can also begin to believe in our own capabilities.

What, then, is remarkable in this scenario of Figure 7.4 is that the Admin team has consistently over a long period of time been more motivated – more energised – than ABS as a whole. And not to get lost in detail here, apart from Year 1, where they were the second most highly motivated team, in the three other succeeding years, they were the most highly motivated! This is quite extraordinary when you think about them being the lowest paid workers in the office. Also, this reminds us of the quotation from Virgil that I cited earlier in this chapter.

This is, so far, simply the motivational scoring, which we know is important. But what about the motivators themselves, which motivators?

	Year 1	Year 2	Year 6	Year 7
ABS Org	63	66	67	62
Admin	75	76	82	71

Figure 7.4 Organisation and Admin motivational scores compared

Activity 7.5

Now review Figure 7.5 which compares the Organisation's motivators over the 4, but non-consecutive, years those of the Admin team. What do you observe and what would you conclude from this comparison?

As always with Motivational Maps, there are so many points that could be made, but we need to focus on the really key ones. First, it is highly apparent that the Organisation and the Admin are in sync regarding their motivators; this is not true of many of the other teams. The Admin team, therefore, are having their motivational energies reinforced not specifically by the management but by the whole organisation. This is like an invisible coating or net that draws them in the same direction as all the people in the company, and so strengthens their sense of purpose or meaningfulness – hence their reinforced belief in the rightness of what they are doing.

Second, we notice that the three core motivators are Searcher, Defender and Expert, and in that order of importance. So far as being an Admin team is concerned this fits almost perfectly with the kind of work they need to do: the Searcher is customer focused, and here their customer is the whole organisation, which it serves. But almost as importantly, the Admin – if no-one else – has to be systems orientated and procedurally driven, which is very much what the Defender wants to do. Finally, given the range of activities that this Admin team has to cope with – from IT in all its ramifications, to filing, researching, invoicing, and HR functions – then the need

TEAM	YEAR	MOTIVATOR POSITION			
		1ST	2ND	3RD	LOWEST
ABS Org	1	Searcher	Defender	Expert	Director
Admin	1	Searcher	Defender	Expert	Director
ABS Org	2	Searcher	Defender	Expert	Director
Admin	2	Searcher	Defender	Builder	Director
ABS Org	6	Searcher	Defender	Expert	Director
Admin	6	Searcher	Defender	Expert	Director
ABS Org	7	Searcher	Expert	Defender	Star
Admin	7	Searcher	Expert	Defender	Director

Figure 7.5 Organisation and Admin motivators compared

for ongoing professional development is critical. In other words, the Expert motivator.

Third, and finally here, let's comment on something more problematic. In terms of belief we note that not only are the top three motivators more or less completely aligned (in Years 1 and 6 they are exactly the same) but so also is the Lowest motivator, which with one exception (the Organisation in Year 7 which has Star) remains the Director. That they are aligned even here is good from the point of view of belief, because particularly this motivator – the Director – can be very disruptive to other motivational types, since it tends to want to take control. Imagine the situation whereby the Admin team came under the influence of strong Director types seeking to control its activities when this kind of behavior was something they actually disliked. How would that play out? On the other hand, with the whole organisation, as well as the Admin team specifically, having a very weak drive to manage, control and take responsibility, can that be a good thing? Actually, as events proved in this case, no. In one hyphenated word, we find too much 'laissez-faire'.

So we need to dig deeper here to uncover more of what is going on. And it needs to be said at this point, in giving more background information, that this team experienced a strange contradiction but one that is not that uncommon in SMEs. First, it needs to be pointed out that the work in this company took place over more than a 10-year period.[21] During that time, whilst all the employees, including the senior directors of the company, were Map profiled regularly, the MD – the major shareholder of the company – declined to be mapped! He wanted to know everyone else's profile, but not be known himself.[22] There were seemingly good reasons for this at the time, but retrospectively one realises this was – potentially – a mistake to permit. However, given this anomaly, one thing was pretty clear working within the company: that the MD most certainly had Director in his top three motivators, for he could not stop micro-managing everyone around him. All the teams suffered from this, except … you've guessed it, the Admin team! Why? How?

The reason why the MD could not interfere with the Admin team was because the Finance Director (Figure 7.6, Pamela, SMT1)[23] was a strong individual put in charge of it to start with – and she did not allow interference with her domain! The MD lion could interfere with all the other animals in his jungle, but the lioness and her cubs nobody messed with. This meant that the Admin team could develop without, as we mentioned in our Preface, the Petronius Arbiter syndrome[24] occurring: 'We trained hard … But it seemed that every time we were beginning to form up in teams we would be reorganised. I was to learn later in life that we tend to meet any new situation by reorganising, and a wonderful method it can be for creating the illusion of progress while producing confusion, inefficiency and demoralisation'.

Name		Searcher	Defender	Expert	Builder	Friend	Spirit	Creator	Star	Director	Motivation Audit			
											%	1	2	3
Pamela	SMT 1	23	24	19	21	26	20	12	20	15	98%	10	10	9
Fred		22	23	26	22	6	24	24	16	17	70%	7	7	7
Vicky	MAN 1	20	23	25	21	18	19	21	17	16	90%	9	9	9
Sarah	1	38	32	14	25	22	16	14	7	12	66%	6	9	6
Caroline	1	26	26	26	20	21	12	21	16	12	72%	7	5	10
Rachel		27	24	27	19	28	17	18	15	5	66%	8	6	3
Mia	1	26	26	16	25	19	23	19	15	11	62%	6	8	5
Total		182	178	153	153	140	131	129	106	88	75%			

Figure 7.6 Admin team Motivational Map year 1

If we look at Figure 7.7, we see Pamela still firmly in control, and even more highly motivated!

The team is changing – Fred and Rachel have left, but there has only been one replacement, Jane. We might note that the departure of Fred is probably not surprising; he is reasonably motivated, but his profile is at odds with the team, and he is the only person with Spirit in his top three. Given this team profile, that does not seem a fit. Rachel's top motivator does not really fit either, although it did mean that her relationship with Pamela was warm. But her motivational scores, relative to the team, were the lowest except for Mia. Mia was a part-timer who actually was much older than anybody else in the team, was 'old school', and was in the team through an historical anachronism – and would soon retire anyway. The addition of Jane, motivationally, was largely consistent with the team profile: although in Year 2, Builder has replaced Expert as third motivator, a cursory examination shows this to be because of Mia's Builder spike – she alone has it in her top three, and approaching retirement presumably has it weighing on her mind more than her younger counterparts.

Overall, the motivational score has improved by 1%: from 75% to 76%. However, we need to examine this more closely.

Name		Searcher	Defender	Builder	Expert	Spirit	Friend	Creator	Star	Director	Motivation Audit %	1	2	3
Vicky	MAN 2	20	20	20	20	20	20	20	20	20	100%	10	10	10
Caroline	2	26	22	16	23	18	21	20	15	16	52%	5	7	4
Jane	1	32	22	18	24	16	8	26	19	15	80%	8	8	8
Mia	2	27	22	34	20	24	17	18	11	7	54%	5	8	4
Sarah	2	40	29	23	26	17	15	7	16	7	70%	7	7	7
Pamela	SMT 2	20	27	23	17	23	25	12	16	17	100%	10	10	10
Total		165	142	134	130	118	106	103	97	82	76%			

Figure 7.7 Admin team Motivational Map year 2

Activity 7.6

Comparing Figures 7.6 and 7.7, what in your opinion might be a cause for concern in the motivational scoring?

Four factors increase the overall scoring in Year 2: first, the addition of Jane, who is 80% motivated which is above the average for Year 1. Two, Sarah's score has slightly increased. And three and four, we have both the SMT leader, Pamela and the manager, Vicky, now scoring 100%. Their scores may be valid, so that is all good, but keep in mind that they are the leaders. Caroline and Mia, however, have both seriously lost motivation. Furthermore, despite being 100% motivated, Vicky has effectively no motivators at all! Note her scoring: all motivators are 20/20 – exactly, so that although there is a technical result or order, in reality all nine motivators are pulling her equally. This suggests that the demands on the team are coming from all angles and – protean-like – Vicky is able to respond with equanimity, as it were, and not be motivationally phased. A cool hand steering the ship. However, there is clearly turbulence,[25] and the lower scores of Caroline and Mia reflect that.

But what has this got to do with belief? We have to be tentative here, because so many factors are and can be involved. But look at stability: two personnel changes and major, de-motivating turbulence, and yet the motivational scores remain steady; and perhaps even more revealingly, the motivational profile is more or less constant. Indeed, without Mia's extreme and non-representative spike on Builder, the two team maps would be the same for their top three and lowest motivators: this is a team built on the energies of Searcher, Defender and Expert. In one sense, since they are so stable despite all that is happening, they come to embody beliefs about themselves: we believe we make a difference, we believe in proper systems and processes, and we value expertise and learning.

As these energies drive forward, so the beliefs in them deepen: beliefs shift attitudes,[26] which generate thoughts and feelings that finally affect decisions and choices. Therefore, a loop – in this case virtuous – emerges whereby the identity of the team is preserved. Now it is important to be clear: sometimes, in order to be effective, a team needs a new infusion of people and different motivators. Diversity can be useful, can be good. But in periods of turbulence, stability can also be a strength, which is what we find here.

Remember what we said before? The essence of belief in teams comes down to this essential point: we believe that teams are more productive than any individual can be. That was the point of the NASA exercise demonstration: to get the individuals to realise that simply in the area of decision-making teams worked better than individuals. Now we are talking about the energies – the motivations – forming a collective impact, which, if they are effective, feed back into the team belief loop.

How, then, does this play out in future? Let's skip a few years and travel to the point where we are close to the end. In Figure 7.8(i) and (ii) we see Years 6 and 7. In other words, we have skipped 4 years to see what has happened with this team, and we are looking to see whether the motivational profiles tell us anything about the team beliefs.

Activity 7.7

Given the thread of what we have been discussing – how motivations might reinforce belief in teams – and from what we have seen in Years 1 and 2 (Figures 7.6 and 7.7), identify three issues relating to these topics from Figures 7.8(i) and (ii) (showing Years 6 and 7).

Before identifying three key issues, let's first clear some ground. Pamela has stepped back from managing this team altogether; she is still in the company, but her role is now exclusively financial. This means Vicky has had to step up and manage – a role Pamela inducted her into. Next, we note that Vicky and Caroline span all four maps, and since joining in Year 2, Jane also has been constantly a member. In fact, in Year 7 there is only one entirely new member, Tina. Depending where we make the cut, we have approximately 50% of the staff who stay in the team. What, then, are three issues that these Maps reveal?

Name		Searcher	Defender	Expert	Friend	Creator	Star	Spirit	Builder	Director	Motivation Audit		
											%	1	2	3
Vicky	MAN 3	25	26	26	18	17	17	20	16	15	86%	8	10	9
Caroline	3	27	27	28	26	16	11	16	14	15	76%	8	7	7
Fiona	1	22	23	16	20	18	25	19	18	19	88%	9	8	9
Hannah	1	27	21	19	25	13	20	16	22	17	80%	8	9	7
Jessica	1	27	18	19	35	19	20	10	19	13	74%	9	3	7
Jane	2	25	25	20	0	35	25	35	8	7	92%	9	9	10
Total		153	140	128	124	118	118	116	97	86	82%			

Figure 7.8(i) Admin team Motivational Map year 6

Name		Searcher	Expert	Defender	Creator	Friend	Star	Spirit	Builder	Director	Motivation Audit		
											%	1	2	3
Vicky	MAN 4	21	25	25	20	18	16	19	22	14	94%	9	10	10
Caroline	4	31	31	28	15	26	8	17	12	12	70%	7	8	6
Tina		29	17	25	20	20	18	17	18	16	60%	6	5	7
Fiona	2	27	16	25	21	21	19	15	19	17	90%	9	9	9
Hannah	2	26	22	15	17	19	20	19	20	22	74%	7	8	8
Jane	3	25	33	19	28	9	25	20	8	13	74%	7	8	8
Jessica	2	20	34	23	22	17	19	16	17	12	40%	3	8	3
Total		179	178	160	143	130	125	123	116	106	71%			

Figure 7.8(ii) Admin team Motivational Map year 7

First, and perhaps most importantly, the team motivational profile remains amazingly stable: we have Searcher, Defender and Expert in Years 6 and 7 as we did in Year 1 and, more or less, in Year 2. And the Director motivator still remains lowest in all four years. This consistency over 7 years might suggest a too comfortable arrangement; what we like to call a Country Club scenario whereby nobody disturbs the status quo.

However, this seems – and is – unlikely in this situation because – second issue – the motivational scoring is persistently high, peaking in Year 6 at 82% – in the Optimal Zone of motivation. Usually Country Club scenarios have, at best, scores in the middling 50–60% range. That said, the drop to 71% in Year 7 is slightly concerning, though we note that the whole ABS organisational motivation also drops to 62% (see Figure 7.4). Is something going on here?

The answer is yes. And here we come to a highly advanced application of Motivational Maps that can be extraordinarily powerful. I'd like to introduce you to some of the concepts here, albeit space is brief, and clearly what I am about to show is just the beginning: a whole book of case studies could be written on this topic. I am talking about the satisfaction rating scores and how they apply collectively, that is, across a team.

For example, if we take Vicky in Year 7 (Figure 7.8(ii)) and see that her top three motivators are Expert, Defender and Builder, we also see that her satisfaction ratings with these 3 motivators are respectively, 9, 10, 10 (all out of 10 maximum). In other words, Vicky is 100% satisfied that her Defender and Builder motivators are being met at work, but only 90% satisfied with her top motivator, the Expert. But what instead of looking at the individual's satisfaction, we attempted to review the overall satisfaction of a specific motivator?

Take the Expert motivator in Year 7 (Figure 7.8(ii)). Who has this motivator in their top three? Vicky, Caroline, Hannah, Jane and Jessica. We might represent this information in this way, Figure 7.9.

Number	Name	Rank	Score/10
1	Vicky	1st	9
2	Caroline	2nd	8
3	Hannah	2nd	8
4	Jane	1st	7
5	Jessica	1st	3
		TOTAL	35
		AVERAGE= /number:5	7

Figure 7.9 Calculating a motivator team satisfaction score

On its own, this information is interesting but limited. We know that the Expert motivator is important to this team in Year 7: it's ranked second, although in reality we might want to consider it first.

Activity 7.8

Study Year 7 in Figures 7.8(i) and (ii). Why might we think that Expert is actually more important in this team than the Searcher, which seems to be the top motivator?

The reason why this may be the case, and something senior management would do well to ponder, is that there is – with seven team members – only a one point difference in the scoring: Searcher 179 versus Expert 178, but the Expert motivator is in the top three of five team members, whereas the Searcher motivator is only in the top three of four team members. It is the averaging effect of the non-top three scores that leads to the Searcher coming out first.

But be that as it may, what we are learning is that in Year 7 the Admin team is reasonably satisfied (7/10) that their learning needs are being met. Since 6/10 would be an 'average' score, then 7 is better, but clearly not ideal. What we need, though, is to see how all the satisfaction scores of the leading motivators stack up. Figure 7.10, then, takes the three motivators that consistently span the 7 years, as shown in Figure 7.5, and applies the process we have outlined in Figure 7.9.

Now we begin to see, in Figure 7.10, some information with much wider implications.

Activity 7.9

What implications might you draw out from Figure 7.10? What might be helpful in terms of thinking about top performing teams and in terms of team belief?

The first thing that seems important is that the satisfaction ratings for the motivators are quite consistent, but their tendencies are going in different directions. The Searcher is consistently around the 7+ score and

Year	Searcher	Defender	Expert
Y1	7.8	8.8	6.0
Y2	7.6	8.0	6.3
Y6	7.2	8.8	8.0
Y7	7.3	7.6	7.0

Figure 7.10 Satisfaction ratings Admin team years 1, 2, 6 and 7

the Defender around the 8+ score, but the overall direction seems to be downwards: a small and slight erosion in the sense of accomplishing mission and in feeling secure is detectable in the numbers. This is particularly marked in Year 7 where the Defender drops for the first time to below 8 at 7.6. The making a difference in Years 6 and 7 is not quite as good as in Years 1 and 2. On the other hand, the Expert satisfaction is trending upwards, despite the lapse to 7 in Year 7; for both Years 6 and 7 are ahead of Years 1 and 2.

If we take the numbers and do a little further calculation on them, we then find, in Figure 7.11, that we have even more information.

We see from the Average numbers that Defender (8.3) may not be the top motivator, but it is the most satisfied one. Perhaps this should not surprise us in that there has been a consistency of personnel and leadership over a long period of time. Expert, on the other hand, is the least satisfied of the top three motivators (6.8), but this seems about to change. And it is the Range numbers that indicate this: the making a difference for the customer has changed only in a small way (although now beginning to dip), but the Expert motivator satisfaction rating has increased by a whole 2.0 points (from 6.0 to 8.0 max, which is, 2 of 6, a 33% increase) over the period.

What can we deduce from this? I think we can deduce two opposing conclusions, although from the numbers alone one seems more likely. We discover which conclusion is correct, however, by always referring to what is happening on the ground: how did this top performing team – for that is what they are – pan out?

One conclusion – the less likely one – is that the motivations of the team are changing, and that the desire to make a difference and to get the right processes in place to do so, is being augmented by an increasing desire – hunger even – within the team for more learning and expertise. On the face of it, that seems good; but I think there are good motivational reasons for suspecting this is not the scenario that is unfolding. The primary reason for this is two-fold: namely, that the Expert motivator in Year 7, despite the upward drift from Years 1 and 2, has fallen backwards, and quite significantly (from 8.0 to 7.0); at the same time, the overall motivation has dropped from 82% to 71% (Figure 7.4) AND the sense of security, the Defender motivator, satisfaction rating is also falling away (from 8.8 to 7.6), which is following the general drift downwards. Why would security satisfaction be less if the company were doing well? And if the Admin team 'believed' that to be the case?

	Searcher	Defender	Expert
Range (Y1-Y7: Max - Min scores)	0.6	1.2	2.0
Average (Y1-Y7: totals / 4)	7.5	8.3	6.8

Figure 7.11 Satisfaction range and averages for Admin team over a 7-year period

Here we reach an unpalatable truth about organisational life: namely, that top performing teams can be destroyed, not through any fault of their own but because of other factors within the organisational structure. Of which, of course, poor leadership is the primary reason. Sadly, too, within the hierarchy of most organisations and companies, Admin teams tend not to have a lot of political clout or weight: they are not rain-makers, or profit centres, but costs to the business, and so invariably a last consideration in terms of needs and rewards.

So, the second – and correct interpretation of these numbers (see Endnote 20 for more on the problem) – is that a crisis is looming, despite the excellent work this team is performing. Essentially, the issue is this: both satisfaction with making a difference and feeling secure is waning, and in a situation like that we ask ourselves, why is that? Often the answer we tell ourselves is[27]: I am not performing well enough because I don't know enough. Ergo, I need to know more, develop more expertise, and then my contribution will make that difference and also ensure my – our, the team – security. The Expert motivator, then, can almost in this situation be viewed as a coping motivator – one[28] we easily resort to in any crisis.

Looking at motivators in this way can, therefore, be a massive help in understanding a number of things. Firstly, we have seen that this is a top performing team from the comparisons with organisational results over a long period of time. Second, we learn that satisfaction with motivators can give us a clue, an inkling, into the state of belief in the team and, by extension, the organisation at any given point. We have deliberately here tried to reduce the amount of data presented (omitting Years 3, 4, and 5) in order to keep it manageable. But clearly, patterns emerge that are extremely revealing. Third, and finally for this chapter, it is worth pointing out that it is small changes in the numbers that can be so indicative: the Range numbers, for example, in Figure 7.11 are not large, but comparing them with each other shows wide variations which are meaningful.

At the end of the day, whilst there is not a necessarily direct correlation between team motivation and belief in the team, when we examine the details we see the sort of evidence that shows us what sort of beliefs a team holds and the direction in which those energies are going. If we know that, we know – using Reward Strategy ideas from Chapter 2 – how to provide more fuel and sustenance to keep top performing teams top, and even to revive teams that are flagging.

From here we reach our final chapter on the fourth characteristic of top performing teams: accountability.

Notes

1   For more on this, see *Mapping Motivation*, James Sale (Routledge, 2016), Chapter 6 and Activity 4. Also, see *Mapping Motivation for Leadership*, James Sale and Jane Thomas (Routledge, 2020), Chapter 6 and Activity 6.1.

2 See Mapping Motivation, James Sale (Routledge, 2016), Chapter 2: The Roots of Motivation, for a thorough account of this.

3 William James, *The Will to Believe and Other Essays in Popular Philosophy* (1897), 'Is Life Worth Living?'. Republished (CreateSpace Independent Publishing Platform, 2017).

4 Lynn Picknett and Clive Prince, *Stargate Conspiracy* (Hachette, 1999). GK Chesterton put it this way: 'At least in the mind of man, if not in the nature of things, there seems to be some connection between concentration and reality'. *The Common Man* (Sheed and Ward Inc, 1950).

5 Norman Vincent Peale, *You Can If You Think You Can* (Touchstone, 1987).

6 There are major chapters in our book, *Mapping Motivation for Coaching*, James Sale and Bevis Moynan (Routledge, 2018), exploring this in great detail.

7 As Martin Seligman says, 'It is essential to realise that your beliefs are just that – beliefs. They may or may not be facts'. *Authentic Happiness* (Random House, 2002).

8 We have covered this before, but we like the acronym, T.E.A.M. = Together Each Achieves More. See *Mapping Motivation*, ibid., Chapter 6.

9 John Stuart Mill, from *On Liberty, Utilitarianism, Considerations on Representative Government, and The Subjection of Women* (1861), https://amzn.to/3eITsRN

10 Dr Alan Watkins, *Coherence* (Kogan Page, 2014).

11 The original NASA instructions seem first to have been written up in 'The effects of a normative intervention on group decision-making performance. Human Relations,' by J. Hall and W.H. Watson (1970). They have been replicated all over the world in university and college training courses, as well as in business and organisational environments. A well-known variant of the example we use is a group being trapped in a cave and having to decide on what items to carry to save themselves. We prefer the Moon scenario precisely because no-one in the group will actually have been to the Moon!

12 NASA is The National Aeronautics and Space Administration: an independent agency of the United States Federal Government, which is responsible for the civilian space program, as well as aeronautics and aerospace research.

13 As I write this, I am in the fifth week of the Covid-19 UK lockdown. All organisations in the UK and much the world are now having to face decision-making with a huge number of unknowns before them. Are they going to make these decisions on their own, or are they going to seek to understand what their team, or teams even, think and recommend?

14 NASA also has descriptors for these scores. It's a six-point range, which is not what we normally use; but here are their words for this: 0–25 Excellent: You and your crew demonstrate great survival skill; 26–32 Good: Above average results. Yes, you made it; 33–45 Average: It was a struggle, but you made it in the end; 46–55 Fair: At least you're still alive, but only just; 56–70 Poor: Sadly, not everyone made it back to the mother ship; 71+ Very poor: Your bodies lie lifeless on the surface of the moon. Serious consequences then!

15 Keep in mind, we establish the difference; this is a positive number and there can be no negative numbers – so one can rate the object less or more than NASA does, but the difference is always a positive number. For example, NASA has rated parachute silk as 8th – if you had it 11th, the difference is 3, and if you had it 5th, the difference is still 3 points.

16 A famous commentary on this is attributed to Petronius Arbiter: 'We trained hard ... But it seemed that every time we were beginning to form up in teams we would be reorganised. I was to learn later in life that we tend to meet any new situation by reorganising, and a wonderful method it can be for creating the illusion of progress while producing confusion, inefficiency and demoralisation'.

17 And a good starting point for that is via knowing the motivational profile of the 'offending' individual so that one can at least frame one's proposals in terms of their motivational pull for him or her.

18 A great idea is to combine the NASA experiment with: a) the Team Agreement process to be found in *Mapping Motivation for Leadership*, James Sale and Jane Thomas (Routledge, 2019), Chapter 6; and b) with Motivational Mapping the team as per the ideas contained in *Mapping Motivation*, ibid., Chapter 6. These three great techniques combined provide an ideal and in-depth series of analyses that can really rocket launch an underperforming team into its opposite.

19 Another translation of this is: 'They can because they think they can', Possunt quia posse videntur, which even more pointedly refers to belief. From the *Aeneid*, Book 5, line 231.

20 *Mapping Motivation for Leadership*, ibid., see Chapter 5 especially and what leaders do.

21 And to be even clearer: The Mapping company were not called in for a strategic overhaul; it was very much at what might be called an 'arm's length' arrangement. The MD and the senior team were fascinated by the Motivational Maps and the insights they provided, but they were always resistant to the changes suggested that directly affected them personally. Thus, Motivational Maps were highly effective in sponsoring tactical changes: for example, in recruitment, in motivating specific teams and individuals, and in widening the scope of the organisation's Reward Strategies. But the Maps were not allowed to influence the company at the strategic level. Two years after Maps had stopped working with the company (because they recognised that they could not help further with the limitations imposed on their work), it collapsed as a direct result of its leadership structure – something the Maps had consistently flagged up, but which had never been addressed. This seems to be a reasonably regular phenomenon in the realm of soft skills' training and development: senior management simply refuse to be bound by the rules that govern everybody else, and so organisational cognitive dissonance sets in, which corrodes trust and undermines belief in the remit.

22 For the avoidance of doubt, this happens at corporate levels too! A FTSE 250 company that we worked with recently had the major shareholder declining to be mapped – but everyone else had to be!

23 SMT is the Senior Management Team. The 1 means she only appears in one of the four Admin team maps that occur. Vicky with MAN1 appears also as 2, 3 and 4 – in all the teams in fact. The MAN is the fact that she is the Manager of the team, although in the first case, under the authority of the Finance Director.

24 There is some dispute as to whether these are his words: according to https://bit.ly/2YezEBn they are falsely attributed to Gaius Petronius Arbiter. The quote is from Charlton Ogburn, Jr. (1911–1998), in *Harper's Magazine*, 'Merrill's Marauders: The truth about an incredible adventure' (Jan 1957). However, the principle holds true and I imagine everyone who has had real world work experience recognises, ruefully, its accuracy.

25 In order to ensure anonymity of this case study, we are keen not to reveal which years specifically these team maps represent; only in talking of turbulence it would not be wrong to think that this particular team map corresponds to the effects of the financial crisis of the first decade of the century.

26 See *Mapping Motivation for Coaching*, ibid., Chapter 7.

27 As opposed to blaming others – the management, the leadership, the company et al. – which is what a low-performing team would automatically do.

28 Naturally, it is not the only possible motivator we might want to consult in a crisis. For example, the Friend motivator may well be how many people/teams attract aid and support in difficult times. Or, the Creator motivator, whereby we 'innovate' our way through difficulties. The point here, however, that these two are not in the top three, whereas the Expert is, and so is an easy fit to the team's natural inclination.

Chapter 8

Accountability and top performing teams

We started in Chapter 1 at addressing the question of 'What is a Team?' and we came up with four defining qualities which teams had. Indeed, by virtue of having these qualities we create what we think of as a top performing team, as opposed to simply a group of people calling themselves a 'team'. Throughout our investigation we have attempted, unusually, to keep our focus wherever possible on the topic of motivation and it might be a key component of each of these four qualities. Given the limited space in a book of this size, we have had to omit many aspects of Remit, Interdependency, Belief and Accountability that are not specifically motivational, but we persistently return to the importance of motivation in all these domains.

Figure 8.1 shows the final quality or attribute of a top performing team: being accountable. As we said in Chapter 1, this is about being accountable to each other, and also being accountable to the whole organisation.

Figure 8.1 Being Accountable

In the first instance, as we have said, being accountable to each other is primarily about being able to rely on and trust each other. It should be obvious that this issue has, in some important senses, already been covered in various sections of this book. It was raised in Chapter 1; Chapter 5 dealt with the values we insist on, and reliability and trust clearly need to be explicitly so; Chapter 6 dealt with interdependency, which also has trust implications; and finally in Chapter 7 our beliefs, especially in the efficacy of team themselves, affect our ability to trust one another.

What is less evident in what we have covered so far is the accountability to the whole organisation. This, of course, is primarily to prevent independent fiefdoms emerging, turf wars erupting, and that general politicking occurring which saps motivation, detracts from customer service, and leads to confusion, followed by ultimate organisational failure.

Activity 8.1

How do organisations 'normally', or 'typically', deal with the issue of team accountability? How effective is this? What improvements might you suggest to deal with it?

The usual solutions to accountability are based on improving communication processes and systems; often this means ensuring that the goals and targets, or success criteria, are not lost sight of, as so frequently they are.[1] Patrick Lencioni[2] identifies three in particular: the publication of Goals and Standards, Simple and Regular Progress Reviews and Team Rewards. Lencioni calls these 'a few classic management tools that are as effective as they are simple'. And we agree. In fact, we believe in Chapter 2 of this book we have added – motivationally – to what team rewards might be.

But what else – especially motivationally – might lead to greater team accountability? The idea of simple and regular progress reviews is excellent and needs to be extended to include motivation – specifically, how motivationally is our team doing versus the rest of the organisation and other teams? To be able to do this is relatively straightforward through using The Organisational Motivational Map.[3]

Figure 8.2 shows us the teams within a division of a large organisation. The approximate size, in total, is over 200 staff. What Figure 8.2 shows is the motivational scores of each team set beneath two crucial benchmarks: first, along the top, the overall score for the whole division; second, the Leaders' team, the score for the senior management team who are managing the six teams below them. It is important to note just where the teams score relative to the 60% score, since falling below 60% puts the team in the second quadrant (or zone, see Figure 2.1), which is 'Risk'.

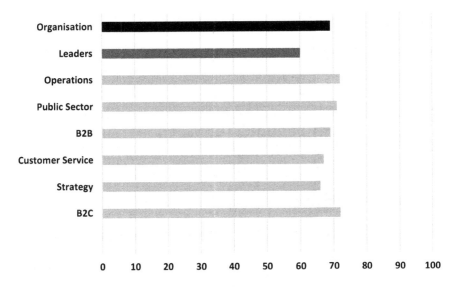

Figure 8.2 Motivational quadrant distribution of an organisational division

Activity 8.2

Given the set-up outlined in the previous paragraph, what is the single most important observation or conclusion you would draw from studying Figure 8.2? And is there anything else you would comment on?

The single – and alarming – most important factor in this chart is that the leaders of the teams – the senior management team, in short – are less motivated than the teams themselves! This, as we have often commented in the Mapping Motivation series of books,[4] is always a bad sign. Staff take their lead from their leaders, and if the leaders are less motivated, then at some future point employees will revert to being more like them. That is, less motivated; for why be otherwise?

And, of course, the question – why be otherwise? – indicates a lack of accountability on the part of the leaders. Until the Organisational team map threw up this result, they weren't even aware of the problem, or what its longer term consequences might be. But our energy levels, our motivation, are our responsibility – we have to set an example to those we manage, and hold ourselves accountable to a higher standard than a mere job description.

One other point we might comment on is the fact that all the teams in this example are in the same quadrant: the Boost Zone of 61–80%. The exception is the Leader team at 60%, but that is still so close as to be marginal. What this suggests is good news: that at the least there is a motivational coherence, or approach, running through the whole organisation. Keeping a close eye on motivational variation can help sustain that pattern.

Organisation Motivation Score: 69%
Range of Scores: 9.4
Change Index Score: 66%
RAG: 31-31-38

Team Name	Searcher	Expert	Spirit	Defender	Creator	Builder	Star	Friend	Director	Motivation Audit %
Operations	736	675	665	611	677	563	477	552	444	72%
Public Sector	526	392	518	400	441	454	391	311	347	70%
B2B	365	293	256	306	283	331	256	191	239	69%
Customer Services	567	531	468	515	430	359	355	412	323	67%
Leaders	229	199	188	172	161	177	178	164	152	60%
Strategy	101	99	86	91	77	59	71	82	54	66%
B2C	102	84	90	68	81	76	67	59	93	72%
Scoring Totals	2626	2273	2271	2163	2150	2019	1795	1771	1652	
PMA Total	736	785	687	699	682	626	683	737	699	
PMA %	71%	75%	66%	67%	66%	60%	66%	71%	67%	
PMA Rank	3	1	6	4	8	9	7	2	5	

Information Classification: General

Figure 8.3 Teams in a division of the organisation

If, then, we take this further, what do these particular teams look like (omitting the whole organisation for now)?

This comparison of team maps now contains some vital and extra[5] information which needs explanation. We see three extra rows at the bottom of the chart – called PMA Total, PMA% and PMA Rank – that look unfamiliar. What are they, and what are they telling us? These are available in the Organisational Motivational Map.

First, the 'PMA Total' is showing us the combined scores of satisfaction rating for each individual motivator. To make this simple: suppose we had a team of two people, Peter and Susan. Peter's satisfaction for his Searcher motivator in his profile was 6/10 and Susan's was 8/10. Then their PMA Total would be 14 (out of 20). Which means that their 'PMA%' would be 70% (in other words, the average). Finally, we might ask how that number compared with the other eight satisfaction numbers, and then rank them accordingly: the 'PMA Rank'. Imagine now, then, that process involving dozens, hundreds or even thousands of people. Indeed, the bigger the number sampled the more accurate and to the point the results are going to be.

To be even clearer: this PMA Rank order is not the same as the Motivational type rank order; for as we see in Figure 8.3, the Searcher is the most important motivator, that is, it is number 1, BUT in terms of its satisfaction it only ranks 3rd!!! This discrepancy (or not) between what the rank order of the motivators is and what the rank order of their satisfaction is, thus throws up the possibility of some fascinating insights into what is going on at team and organisational level. Furthermore, it also leads directly into a form of accountability: specifically, from the team leaders and from the whole organisation (or division).

Activity 8.3

What in your view might be some of the insights or ideas that emerge from contrasting the two rank orders of motivators versus satisfaction?

Perhaps the most important insight to emerge might be whether or not the employees are likely to be engaged, based on their motivators, and whether or not the ones that are most important are actually being satisfied. Given that these are aggregated scores, they are going to be very accurate. Second, are the team leaders and the organisation itself actually targeting their reward strategies effectively? And if not, then potentially, this information could give them precision as to where the real need or want is. Thirdly, at the lower end of the motivational spectrum, where we might encounter what we call 'hygiene factors',[6] is this exacerbated or ameliorated by the satisfaction ratings? In other words, is there a looming crisis here that the satisfaction ratings might flag up?

Activity 8.4

Given what we have just said, study Figure 8.3 and come up with three key perceptions and three recommendations for action. As you look at these numbers, what are you seeing that might be helpful in improving the performance and capability of these teams? Keep in mind as well that the team maps are a form of accountability.

Three key perceptions that immediately strike one might be: that all seen teams have Searcher as their number one motivator. This suggests a strong corporate ethos and culture informing the long-term as well as the day-to-day running of the organisation. However, there is also a question to be asked: are the motivators too homogenous? In other words, is there enough diversity?

Secondly, and noticeably, however, we find, as we did in the high performing Admin team in Chapter 7, that Director is the lowest motivator collectively; and with four teams it is specifically lowest. (We note, too, in passing one small detail that might need examining: one team, B2C, has the Director motivator as its second highest motivator – how do they interact with the others?)

Finally, and drawing on the new information of PMA scores we have added and expounded, we notice that the rank order of the motivators is not the same as the rank order of the satisfactions. In fact, it is wildly variant. To mention three striking divergences here: The Searcher is only the third satisfied motivator; the lowest motivator, Director, is in fact ranked 5th in terms of satisfaction; and perhaps, most incredible of all, The Friend motivator, ranked 8th, is actually 2nd in terms of job satisfaction!!! So what does this all mean, and what are the recommendations for action that emerge from it?

If we look at Figure 8.4 we get an overview of the data that are in Figure 8.3. We see on the vertical axis the motivators aligned in their hierarchical positions, and along the horizontal axis, we see the nine satisfaction rankings. So that Expert is ranked first overall in terms of its being satisfied. But what does this suggest?

Again, being clear that there is always a certain amount of ambiguity inherent in motivational 'readings' or interpretations, this would indicate that although the employees overall are committed most of all to making a difference for the customer/clients that they have, the resources of the organisation are more effectively channeled into training, learning and development opportunities. Now this may be because, strategically, the management quite consciously think that through 'training' (understood in its widest sense, which would include 'L&D')[7] they are best able to satisfy the customers' needs and so make that difference or fulfil their mission. But notice those small words, 'this may be'. Of course, it may not be. It may be easier – especially for professional service type people, as these are – to run training courses and complete Personal Development Plans (PDPs) than to undertake the seriously difficult task of satisfying the customer – see Figure 3.1! And it is certainly a lot more straight forward. Let's keep this issue hanging for a moment.

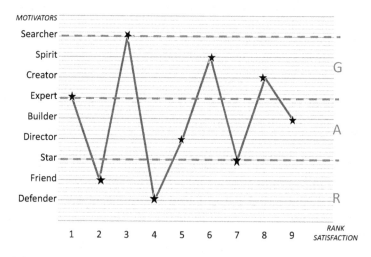

Figure 8.4 Rank motivators, rank satisfactions

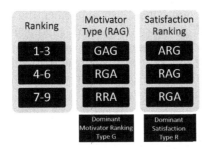

Figure 8.5 The dominant RAG

For if we take this further, drill down on the data to another level, we get to a point where we can answer this issue with more certainty.

Taking the information from Figure 8.4 and then re-processing it in Figure 8.5, we find the following: that the dominant motivational cluster is the G or Growth motivators. This is obvious because we see that two Growth motivators are in the top three, as well as the third one appearing in the second tier or row as 5th most important. Of course, we need only look at Figure 8.3 as well to see the RAG scores are: 31(R)–31(A)–38(G). Definitely, then, Growth motivators dominate this division. But what about the PMA scores: which type of motivators are dominantly satisfied?

A simple way of looking at this would be to remember that being a satisfied motivator is not hierarchical as the motivators themselves are. So we can give points for being 1st (3), 2nd (2), or 3rd (1) to get a sense of what is most significant here,[8] as we do in Figure 8.6.

From this we see that although the Growth motivators are more important to the employees, it is the Relationship motivators that are being satisfied

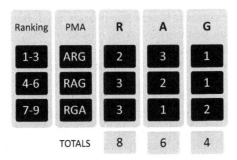

Figure 8.6 Dominant PMA

more effectively. This suggests – to return to the issue we left hanging – that the management are not consciously implementing a strategy, but rather that the culture itself is determining what is happening. In this sense, the motivational – and so engagement – drive of the teams is less than optimal. Indeed, we need to stop what we are doing and do a thorough review of the whole division/organisation to explore exactly how this has come about and how, exactly, it is manifesting itself.[9]

But if we now look at what needs addressing immediately, and so answer the second part of our own question, which is, what three recommendations for action would one take, then it seems the following is clear.

The Spirit motivator is in the top three, but its satisfaction rating is only 6th. So, we need to address – using Reward Strategies – how we can loosen the constraints of time and decision-making within the whole division. See the Resources section and Figure 1.8 for more on specific rewards for the Spirit Teams. But three ideas from that list which spring immediately to mind and might be relevant here are:

1. *Increase the scope of the Spirit team's decision-making. Delegate to them, where appropriate. Reduce 'interference' in how they work.*
2. *Let Spirit team members work at home! This is particularly the case where the technology and the role coincide. It is also an increasingly relevant factor following the worldwide Covid-19 Pandemic.*[10]
3. *Allocate 10% of time – one afternoon a week – to allow Spirit teams to work on their own projects and research which may benefit the organisation.*

It is perhaps worth mentioning here that these Spirit motivator type of Reward Strategies are highly aligned with the way that many experts think organisational life is going. Professor Gary Hamel,[11] for example, points out that it, 'Turns out you don't need a lot of top-down discipline when four conditions are met: 1. First-line employees are responsible for results; 2. Team members have access to real-time performance data; 3. They have decision authority over the key variables that influence performance outcomes; 4. There's a tight coupling between results, compensation, and recognition'. This 'loosening' of controls is very Spirit-orientated, but we need to be clear that whereas it may be desirable generally, there are motivator types that require the exact opposite!

Second, Builder is the 6th most important motivator, so it is not really significant; but it is also not insignificant, and when we notice that its satisfaction ranking is 9th, then this is a clear warning that the staff feel underpaid. They have other benefits that are satisfying them – training and development: for example, the Expert – but in the long term this might lead to staff turnover and difficulties in attracting the right calibre of personnel. We need to review our Total Rewards Model – see Figures 2.7 and 2.8. What can we do here?

Third, we must never forget that the first motivator is the first motivator, and as this is only being satisfied at a lower perception level than two others, then this ought to be addressed. How do we reinforce mission, get staff to feel they are making a difference, and in short, address the Remit question? We note that part of the answer is discussed in our Chapter 3; and we note, too, that the comments on the Relationship motivators are also perhaps relevant here – given the low scoring of the Friend, but the high scoring for its satisfaction rating. We might want to ask how that internal bonding might be projected externally to our customers?

If we take all these rather simple things combined, we have a recipe – an experimental recipe – for making a series of small changes which collectively can make a big impact on the performance of the teams, and on their ongoing accountability to the whole organisation. It's important to say 'experimental' recipe because as we constantly emphasize: motivation and how people react to stimuli and interventions can be unpredictable. But doing nothing is not an option: as Zig Ziglar[12] commented, 'People often say that motivation doesn't last. Well, neither does bathing – that's why we recommend it daily'.

In this case example the motivational score within six to nine months of the interventions for the whole cohort of seven teams moved from 69% to 73%, a shift of 4%. This sounds small, but over a large number of employees, this is significant; all the more so because as we approach the Optimal Zone of motivation (at 81%) it becomes more difficult to extract more energy from the staff. This is exactly analogous to athletes or sports people. If we have done no exercise whatever, then small steps initially can lead to vast improvements in one's ability to run the 100 metres. However, as one gets closer and closer to the world record time,[13] then gains become more and more difficult. But it is persistence that pays off: we saw in Chapter 7 how Motivational Maps impacted a team over a 7-year period, and this despite a leadership that was less than effective. The prize before us is this: increases in motivation lead to increases in performance, which themselves lead to increases in productivity; ultimately, these increases in productivity will produce – if the organisation has the right strategy for producing, disseminating its products and services – increased profitability.

So seeing how teams, motivationally, compare with each other within an organisation is clearly vitally important in terms not only of performance, but also of accountability. This is easy, inexpensive data to access and to act upon. But if, therefore, comparing teams within an organisation is a form of accountability, so too is tracking the motivational changes for a specific team. We did this in Chapter 7 with the Admin team of ABS Ltd. Let's now expand these data significantly to see how this helps and what results it might lead to.

The context is an Insurance company in the first decade of this century facing the reality that things have changed. After 30 years of making a profit by simply 'being there', the new reality is: changing technology, enhanced customer service expectations, increased competition, and industry consolidation. In other words, an old-school business now seeking to play catch-up. Into this situation a new dynamic MD seeks to develop a high performance culture, delight customers with levels of service exceeding their competitors, drive brand awareness, double the volume of business and increase profitability. This she was able to do (so we will forego discussing results specifically, as we wish to stick with motivational issues) and shortly afterwards there followed a buy-out, another consolidation, and the MD being 'poached' to become equally effective elsewhere.

Thus, we are in a fast-moving change environment, which of course has only accelerated since then, although the principles remain the same. Not only has the MD now gone, but along the way there were many changes of staff personnel. One of the primary concerns in July 07 was to retain quality staff and develop them to reverse the attrition rate and its cost to the business. Given that the targets were met over the 3-year period, what does a snapshot of the motivational information tell us?

Activity 8.5

The motivational profiling was to occur every 3 months during the change period. But clearly that didn't quite go to plan – events intruded. What, though, do the motivational scores over five significant intervals of time tell us? And why might that be even more remarkable if we consider the years in question, especially 2007/8?[14] An event that intruded?

What we see of course is what we most want to see: the company is making steady but significant progress in its overall staff motivation, and this is all the more remarkable since it occurred alongside the financial crisis of 2007/8, but which hit them hardest in 2008 as its effects filtered down into the real economy. Part of the reason for choosing this case study, as opposed to more recent ones, is because with the Covid-19 pandemic (I am in lockdown as I write this) proving to be a bigger financial threat than the 2007/8 crisis, it seems relevant to see how a medium-sized[15] company coped with this on a motivational level. As we come out of lockdowns, all organisations are going to have to cope with the motivations – or lack thereof – of their staff, and its concomitant, performance. But here it's not just the 5 percentage points of 57% to 62% that is significant: it is the Zone they cross. 57% is in the Risk Zone (see Figure 2.1), which means that performance is

	0707	0907	0108	0708	1008
ORGANISATION	57%	60%	61%	61%	62%

Figure 8.7 Five consecutive organisational motivation scores

	0707	0907	0108	0708	1008
ORGANISATION	57%	60%	61%	61%	62%
ADMIN	65	70	69	60	52
BUSINESS MAN	*	*	72	77	74
CLAIMS	51	58	56	58	63
RENEWALS	*	55	48	58	56
FINANCE	51	60	51	53	69
KEY ACCOUNTS	*	60	51	60	66
OPERATIONS	68	44	51	45	42
SMT	57	67	68	63	67
SALES	46	58	66	73	68
UNDERWRITING	69	67	74	77	74

Figure 8.8 The organisational team results
* Valid comparison not possible because of re-organisations, changes in personnel, and other factors. In the case of Business Management, this was an entirely new team, led by a new recruit who joined the SMT. At interview, all short-listed candidates completed a Map which was used in the selection process.

on average 'good'. However, good here really means 'average', even medio-cre (see Chapter 2 and Figure 2.6 especially). However, 62% is in the Boost Zone where performance is more likely to be excellent (across the board, as it were). It would be just as significant for the motivational scores to go from 77% to 82%; at which point, the performance leans towards being outstand-ing, and that obviously would be an ambitious goal for the future.

Despite, therefore, the underlying and precarious economic environment, these motivational results are excellent and pointing in the right direction. Let's drill down further now, and see from the teams how it is made up. Keep in mind that the teams do not have equal numbers of staff in them, and so the organisational averages are calculated from the individual aver-ages, not the team averages.

Activity 8.6

Study Figure 8.8. Which teams are going up motivationally, which are going down, and which are holding their own, or in a kind of 'steady-state'?

If you have done Activity 8.6, you will find the results extremely interest-ing. A good way to set them out is in Figure 8.9. Here we can begin to see what is really important.

TEAMS	DOWN	STEADY-STATE	UP
ADMIN	c.13%		
BUSINESS MAN		√	
CLAIMS			c.12%
RENEWALS		√	
FINANCE			c.18%
KEY ACCOUNTS			c.6%
OPERATIONS	c.26%		
SMT			c.10%
SALES			c.22%
UNDERWRITING			c.5%

Figure 8.9 Teams: down, steady-state, and up

Activity 8.7

What, then, is really important? How does this layout in Figure 8.9 help us understand what is going on, and how we might develop high performing teams?

The first thing that is really useful about the Figure 8.9 layout is that without even looking at the details, we can clearly see that the overall trend is upwards, and much more decisively than the mere movement from 57–62% (Figure 8.7) indicates. The 'up' ticks, as it were, exceed the 'down' and 'steady-state' combined; and in a rough and ready way, the 39% (13+26) down is more than offset by the 73% (12+18+6+10+22+5) up. We can be much more confident that we are doing some highly effective activities.

Also, we see that there are two problem areas – two problem teams – and so we can focus on them. From a senior management point of view, this is manageable. Change can seem overwhelming[16]; everything needs doing at once, especially dealing with employees. But here we have it: if we didn't know already, then the numbers say it all.[17] There are some issues in the Admin and Operations teams. Interestingly, this is the reverse of the Admin team in Chapter 7; here, much more typically, Admin is low-status in hierarchical *and* performance terms. And the Operations team is closely allied with Admin, though hierarchically 'higher'; effectively, they are 'expert' administrators ensuring that the correct documentation, compliance, health and safety, cross-departmental (team) exchanges are coherent, and other issues which lead to behaving in a well-oiled sort of way. Like Admin, they are a cost to the business. Thus, we are establishing a connection between these two departments – teams – that might account for their common motivational down-trend: cost-centres often tend to not be seen as important as profit ones.

Conversely, where is the biggest upward trend? Yippee! In Sales – a dream result for almost any commercial organisation – and performance matched the motivational profile, as sales doubled within the time frame. Sales are important, but are the 'less' important teams being left behind? What do the motivators say?

Before we look at the actual motivators, let's consider the process we call Motivational Triangulation.

What we do in this situation is to take the team with the highest motivational trend, together with the team with the lowest motivational trend, and compare them alongside the organisational results. In this way we cut through the clutter of so much information and get to what might be root issues that we can focus on and analyse effectively.

More specifically, in working on a large change management project with an organisation, we initially benchmark the organisation, in this case MY0707. Then, at agreed periods, we map again after we have made the interventions – coaching, mentoring, consultancy, training etc. – and track how the organisation overall, and the teams specifically, are doing. The triangulation is when we set the most improved and least improved (and that can easily mean, as here, a negative move on the motivation, since change is always resisted)[18] against the progress of the organisational motivation. In this way a certain clarity is achieved.

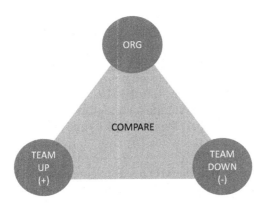

Figure 8.10 Motivational Triangulation

	0707	0907	0108	0708	1008
ORGANISATION	**57**	**60**	**61**	**61**	**62**
1	Defender	Expert	Expert	Builder	Builder
2	Searcher	Defender	Searcher	Searcher	Defender
3	Expert	Searcher	Defender	Expert	Expert
LOWEST MOTIVATOR	Director	Director	Director	Director	Director
OPERATIONS	**68**	**44**	**51**	**45**	**42**
1	Expert	Searcher	Defender	Defender	Defender
2	Builder	Defender	Searcher	Searcher	Searcher
3	Defender	Builder	Expert	Builder	Builder
LOWEST MOTIVATOR	Director	Director	Director	Friend	Director
SALES	**46**	**58**	**66**	**73**	**68**
1	Builder	Expert	Expert	Expert	Expert
2	Searcher	Searcher	Searcher	Builder	Builder
3	Expert	Defender	Defender	Searcher	Defender
LOWEST MOTIVATOR	Director	Director	Director	Friend	Director

Figure 8.11 Motivational Triangulation example

Activity 8.8

By now if you have followed all the Activities in this book, you will be very experienced at spotting the trends that we regard as crucial for helping organisations solve their issues at a deeper level. Figure 8.11, even with all the data from the other teams stripped out, is still a quite complex table. But if you study it, what 'facts' scream out as being highly significant? And how do they help us move these teams and this organisation forward?

First, of course, it needs to be said that one does not wait for five Map readings over a near 18-month period in order to take action; action is taken immediately after the first benchmark (MY0707) is taken. But as we look at this, we see a number of very important factors.

First, we notice that, apart from in the 4th time segment, MY0708, there is a hygiene factor in the fact that the Director motivator is lowest. This clearly will pose problems in the long term, even despite a dynamic MD. The action point from it must be that the MD needs to consider the Director motivator as a factor in all future hires, and especially ones to the senior management team.

Second, the persistent presence (except MY0108) of the Builder motivator in the Operations team must represent a serious mismatch between the remit of the team and its likely rewards. Unlike the Sales team, the Operations staff are not on commission or bonuses, and their remuneration is not at the level of other, more 'prestigious' or 'expert' teams, such as Underwriting. How then can they be satisfied? With the advent of the new MD they expected much, but clearly as the change programme progressed, they became increasingly disappointed. The key issue here is to uncover why the Builder motivator is so persistent; and the answer – revealed through the accompanying coaching programme – proved to be the personal circumstances of two of the members of the team, including its leader.

It is here that great leadership needs to demonstrate itself. An organisation can take the view that this is our pay structure, take it or leave it; or they can personally engage with the people involved. As Binney and Williams[19] observed, 'The personal element is key. When a change agenda shifts from generalities and 'management speak' to individual and collective hopes and fears, expressed in people's own words, then it comes alive and has power'. From this seemingly belated revelation a plan for the team was devised which focused far more on the consequences of successful organisational development, and what that might mean in terms of security, a larger team, and correspondingly bigger rewards. In simple terms, getting them to see the part they were playing in the bigger picture. This worked immediately; we have stopped at MY1008 in order to make the data manageable, but the motivational score for MY0409 for the Operations team was 52%, a significant upturn.

Finally, though much more could be said, MY0708 is obviously a watershed point in the development of the change management programme: the re-entry of the Builder motivator in both the Operations and Sales team, and perhaps most significantly of all, the fact that the Friend motivator has become the lowest motivator for both teams. We see in MY0907 that the change programme is kicking in, at least in an initial phase: The Operations team loses its Expert motivator and the Searcher replaces it – focus on the (internal) customer; whereas the Sales team goes into a major learning phase, which is sustained through all succeeding mapping – indeed, the Sales team experienced a concentrated coaching programme on motivational selling which was quite relentless, because it was so important to the company (doubling turnover). But at MY0708 something extra is happening too: The Director motivator, along with the Builder, is actually moving upwards in both teams. Meaning?

Well, this, of course, is the moment when the financial crisis of 2008 hits the company – the moment of market panic. It's sell or die; perform or die; all hands to the deck. Over and above the change programme, external events were also impacting the day to day working lives of these teams: Friend being lowest is perhaps not entirely desirable, and we have talked about this in Chapter 7. But taking more responsibility (the Director) and being more accountable in the crisis possible is. But it certainly exhausted the Sales team as their motivation dips – though not drastically – in MY1008. At this point, for both Sales and Operational teams, a coaching programme that also involves personal development, well-being and de-stressing components, is essential.

As we reach the end of this chapter, it's important to be clear that in discussing accountability we have not exhausted all or every way of ensuring we have it. But we have considered how motivation and Motivational Maps can give us some astonishing insights into it that normally are not available or even thought of as relevant. We hope you will want to use Maps to track the progress of your teams and to hold them accountable. Don't forget – our first example was of the senior team being accountable for being more highly motivated than most of the other teams!

Notes

1   Colin Hastings writes that, 'Once teams are involved in their tasks it is very easy for them to lose sight of what they are really trying to achieve. Make sure in the first place that all the team fully understand all the subtleties of what is expected of the team. Secondly, make sure that they constantly come back to the key question: what are we trying to achieve and for whom?' – *Teamworking, The Gower Handbook of Management*, Third Edition, Chapter 69 (1992).

2   Patrick Lencioni, *The Five Dysfunctions of Teams* (Jossey-Bass, 2002).

3   See the Resources section for more on the Motivational Organisational Map.

4   Perhaps the most extensive coverage of this is in *Mapping Motivation for Leadership*, James Sale and Jane Thomas (Routledge, 2020), Chapter 7: What Leadership Isn't.

5   This team map first appeared in our *Mapping Motivation for Engagement* book, James Sale and Steve Jones (Routledge, 2019) as Figure 6.3. However, since it was not relevant to that earlier volume, we omitted the PMA Total, PMA%, and PMA Rank scores. Now we can see the extra insight and power these data bring to our analysis.

6   I use the term 'hygiene factor' following the work of Herzberg. Herzberg realised that there were aspects of work which while not motivating in themselves might, through their absence, be de-motivating. For example, nobody is motivated to go to work because of tea and coffee facilities, but if one were to permanently find that the organisation was not interested in providing either refreshments or even a facility where one could make one's own refreshments, this might become extremely de-motivating over time. Frederick Herzberg, The Motivation to Work, 1959, and One More Time, How do You Motivate Employees? *Harvard Business Review*, 1968. As an interesting sidebar, Herzberg clearly had a great sense of humour, for he came up with the KITA formula too: this he identified as how not to motivate and influence people; KITA being an acronym for the 'Kick In The Ass' approach to management!

7   L&D stands for Learning and Development, and this acronym and variants of it are commonplace as departments within most corporates. An article by Mandy Chapman for the *Training Journal* recently (7/1/2020) outlined future prospects for L&D post 2020: https://bit.ly/3dGT7hi

8   Another way of doing this would be to add up the RAG PMA scores and compare them: so G = 2105 (736+687+682), A = 2110 (785+626+699), and R = 2119

(699+683+737). This gives the same result. Either way is useful as a tie-breaker if one method produces a drawn result.

9   Doing this now is beyond the scope of top performing teams per se, but tools, techniques and ideas for investigating what is happening here are contained in two of our previous books: *Mapping Motivation for Engagement*, ibid., and *Mapping Motivation for Leadership*, ibid. In particular, in the former volume, we recommend studying Chapters 6 (Advanced Ideas for Engaging Managers) and 7 (Motivational Organisational Maps and Strategic Narrative); and in the latter volume, Chapters 4 (Leaders Thinking and Planning) and 5 (Leaders Doing). We especially recommend using The Five Elements cycle model we outline, and starting with the C, or Checking questions.

10   See, 'How to profit from the shift towards working from home', Stephen Connolly, *MoneyWeek*, 3/4/2020. Aside from the specific wants of the Spirit motivator, 'According to a 2019 survey in the US ... 80% of employees would like to be able to do so [work from home] at least some of the time, many more than were actually doing so before the advent of Covid-19'.

11   *The Future of Management*, Gary Hamel(Harvard Business School Press, 2007).

12   *Motivation A Key to Success*, Dr Savita Mishra (Lulu, 2017).

13   The current men's world record at the time of writing this is 9.58 seconds, set by Jamaica's Usain Bolt in 2009, while the women's world record of 10.49 seconds set by American Florence Griffith-Joyner in 1988 remains unbroken.

14   Just as this financial institution was waking up to the fact of its eroding position in the market place, and its lack-lustre technology, so the financial crisis of 2007–08, also known as the global financial crisis (GFC), hit. This was a severe worldwide economic crisis and considered by many economists to have been the most serious financial crisis since the Great Depression of the 1930s: https://bit.ly/3cIUpZ7. This of course created a double-whammy for them. Fortunately, they had appointed just the right leader to steer them through this. Hence the motivational scores as well as the results they achieved.

15   They had approximately 80 staff and made a profit of nearly £4M in 2008.

16   And ambiguous: 'Change projects are ambiguous', Donald G Krause, *The Way of the Leader* (Nicholas Brealey Publishing, 1997).

17   As is often the case with consultants or external agencies going into an organisation, senior management is aware that something is 'up', but can't quite put their finger on what it is. This is especially true with the organisational cost centres; in sales or in production, failing targets are highly visible, but with departments – teams – like Administration, the reasons for underperformance can be more difficult to spot.

18   See *Mapping Motivation for Engagement*, ibid., for more on change resistance, especially Chapter 8 and overcoming it.

19   *Leaning into the Future*, George Binney and Colin Williams (Nicholas Brealey, 1995).

Conclusion

We commented in the Preface on how strange it was to be writing a book on motivation and teams when this topic seemed to have been covered so thoroughly before in earlier volumes. For those who have read the four prequels to this volume – congratulations! – you may have noticed something a little different or perhaps more developed in this one: namely, the increased cross-textuality of this book compared with its predecessors. This is manifested in two ways.

First, the number of Endnotes actually referring back to the first four books seems much greater than before. The other books in comparison seem more stand-alone; here, as we press on into deeper levels of motivational understanding, we do need the backstop of earlier ideas, tools and techniques, and the basis on which they were founded. So this makes this book richer and more complex. It can be read on its own, but clearly it's also part of a bigger development of the theme of motivation within team building. Perhaps this should not surprise us: team building is hugely important, and if understanding the dynamics of one person is intricate, then how much more their groupings and gatherings? Let's not forget the reason we want to do this. It can be summed in James Ferguson's observation,[1] referring to the 2012 Olympic Games – 'Team GB came second in the medal table, taking 9% of the medals despite only having 0.8% of the world's population'. In other words, the massive performance and productivity surge that comes when real teams – top performing teams – start taking centre stage.

Second, the cross-textuality also refers to the number of times work or ideas in one chapter elicit a reference to another chapter within the book. To give an example of this: in Chapter 8, dealing with accountability from a motivational perspective, we were able to bypass the issue of accountability to each other by referring back to Chapter 6 and its theme of interdependency. And in this book, this sort of thing is happening all the time. The truth is, that developing a top performing team is a complicated and ambiguous process; and whatever else it is, it is not, and is never going to be, linear. For one thing, change happens. Part of the real difficulty of change goes way beyond the managerial; it is a spiritual matter to perceive what is necessary, of which one aspect is constant sense of alertness and a refusal to be complacent.

The theologian H.A. Williams[2] succinctly captured the essence of the problem when he said: 'Love, for instance, is always looking for new idioms of expression as circumstances change: a son aged twenty is not to be loved in the same way as a son aged five'. We immediately know this to be true – if we have ever loved our child or children. Indeed, we regard as infantile those parents who attempt to keep their children stuck in the nursery of their parenting. But if this is true of children, it is also true of teams: they need nurturing, and to try to treat a team that is 5 years old in exactly the same way we did when they were 5 weeks old is clearly fatuous and ineffective. Teams develop, and if we have done our job (which, incidentally, means we will have developed), then our approach, methods, reward strategies will also reflect that, and rise to the occasion.

Keep in mind what we keep repeating, that this book is about top performing teams from the unique perspective of motivation and Mapping Motivation; it is not therefore the whole story of how one creates a top performing team(s). But the word 'unique' here is important, for as we have established so often in this book and the others in the series, motivation is systematically not addressed when 'experts' consider how such teams are formed. There is lip-service to motivation, but rarely any specifics as to how to go about generating it.

Thus, this book in one sense must not be construed in a linear fashion. The real question might be: where does one start if one wishes to build a top performing team? There can be no easy answer to this question; for one thing, as we have said, the cross-textuality means the issues are 'dense'. But as a conclusion, what should we be thinking about?

If we follow the logic and chapter headings of this book, a modus operandi might emerge. The first thing of all is to consider: do we have a team here or a group? Either way, work will need to be done. In the former case, how effective as a team is it? And in the latter, how do we form a team from this group – what needs to be done? Handily, Chapter 1 shows how using Motivational Maps can help get a clearer picture of your team dynamics and what some of the problems might be.

Then, and this can almost be a standalone itself, we review our reward strategies. Every team, everywhere, is rewarded, even if that is merely being paid the agreed wages. But it should be clear from Chapter 2 that rewards need to be far more wide-ranging: and the understanding of performance's odd, 'disjointed', correlation with rewards is pivotal. As is the idea of the Total Reward Package. And taking into account 'change', how does this change – develop – over time? What are your reward strategies? Remember, 'When rewards are perceived as recognition for competence, they increase intrinsic motivation, probably because they fulfil a psychological need'.[3]

In our view, all the nine motivators can be intrinsic to any given individual, or even team and their sense of identity.

Perhaps the most difficult area of all comes next: The Remit. We have devoted three chapters to the exploration of this topic from a motivational perspective. For some the starting point might well be the customer focus. But keep in mind even with relentless customer focus, Bob Garratt's observation[4] remains true: 'If retention of customers is a key to increased profitability, retention of key people, their experience and developing personal capabilities, is the best way of retaining customers'. The motivation of the staff, then, more generally is the key and we explore this motivationally in a number of ways.

Equally, what we do is part of The Remit, and what the motivators are has a big influence on how well we are going to do it; it also feeds back into what we should be doing. In other words, so that what we are doing and our motivators are aligned. Not to have this alignment would be like accelerating a car with one foot on the brake at the same time; the constant friction would be exhausting, inefficient, and ultimately debilitating. The churn rate of the team would go up, alongside absenteeism and presenteeism.[5] It is a recipe for ultimate failure.

Lastly, on The Remit, we considered the values we insist on, and of particular importance was the PMV tool we discussed and demonstrated. We think this one tool has huge implications for change management, and for developing appropriate strategies even, though the chapter stopped short of that. In essence, the PMV tool encapsulates that wonderful literary critical principle: 'only compare'. How do our motivators, our productivity, our manageability and our values, within a team, compare? And of course, it can be used across teams and for the whole organisation.

After The Remit, we looked at Interdependency in Chapter 6. Here the importance of recruitment surfaced; we need to get the right people on the bus at the start, not once the journey is underway. We saw here how Mapping Motivation could make a massive difference to the recruitment process and increase the chances of getting the right hire. Following on from that, we studied in detail the difference, motivationally, between a high and a low performing team within the same organisation. We identified motivational issues to look for within a team that either strengthened or weakened it.

The penultimate issue was that of Belief. Here we did two things. First, we used a non-motivational tool, the NASA experiment, to help ground belief in the team via this very powerful simulation. Second, we tracked a high performing Administration team over a 7-year period using the Maps. We showed, explained, and discussed in considerable detail how this team was able to retain motivation and performance levels, despite its status within the organisation, and also the overall weak leadership.

Figure C.1 Six motivational steps and choices for your teams

Finally, we came to the Accountability of the team to the whole organisation from a motivational perspective. Here, we'd like to think we came to the highlight of the whole book: namely, the understanding not only of the team motivators, the comparisons of teams through the Organisational Motivational Map, but the satisfaction rankings set against the motivational rankings in order to get completely new insights into what is going on. This advance too, again like the PMV of Chapter 5, has huge potential for change management and to help direct appropriate reward strategies throughout the whole organisation.

If we look at the above, we see whole cornucopia of ideas, techniques and tools that can turn round, as well as fine tune, any team. Remember:

motivation is the fuel that powers the car. Without it, your team is not going anywhere much.

We cannot motivate another human being directly, but we can create the conditions in which their self-motivation is possible; indeed, the team's self-motivation is possible. We must do this because as Andrew Carnegie observed,[6] 'People who are unable to motivate themselves must be content with mediocrity, no matter how impressive their other talents'.

So Figure C.1 provides us with a route map to where we might begin to find some motivational traction to enable us to create and sustain a top performing team. Tom Peters[7] said, 'The amount of performance improvement that is possible from these turned on teams is not small – it is enormous'.

To make things work for us, of course, we have to do 'something', and usually something different from what we have done before. What we have done before may have worked then, but this is now. As I write this the world is in lockdown from Covid-19, and when we come out of it, the world is going to be a different place; work is going to be a different place.[8] We are going to have to work extra hard, and be extra innovative, and be even more bottom-up rather than top-down, if we wish for our teams and organisations to be motivated, engaged and effectively lead. Only in this way, can they be value-driven, profitable and ultimately successful. This requires, therefore, an investment of time, money[9] and effort; and Motivational Maps are the ideal tool to help steer you through this morass of change that is threatening to overwhelm organisations everywhere.

We wish you well as you strive for outstanding performance and the highest levels of motivation in your work and in your life. Now go to the Resources section to find out more about Motivational Maps. May you always be motivated!

Notes

1 James Ferguson, *MoneyWeek*, 26/8/2016.
2 H.A. Williams, *The Joy of God* (Continuum, 1979). This usage of the theological should not surprise Mappers and readers of the earlier books. For example, in *Mapping Motivation for Coaching*, James Sale and Bevis Moynan (Routledge, 2018), Chapter 1, we talk about how listening (what coaches do or should do) is so closely aligned with love and loving someone; and how effective that is in solving particular problems or issues. This accords with our general principle that management needs to be more bottom-up and less top-down.
3 Amar Fall and Patrice Russell, 'Compensation and Work Motivation: Self-Determination Theory and the Paradigm of Motivation through Incentives', in *The Oxford Handbook of Work Engagement, Motivation and Self-Engagement Theory*, edited Marylène Gagné (Oxford University Press, 2014).
4 Bob Garratt, *The Fish Rots from the Head* (HarperCollins, 1997).
5 'Sir Cary Cooper, professor of organisational psychology and health at the Manchester Business School at Manchester University, said that people were frightened of taking time off for sickness, and that presenteeism was a big threat to UK workplace productivity' – http://bbc.in/2yoguaR

6 Andrew Carnegie, cited, *The Epoch Times*, 28/5/2020; also, Paul Bowden, *Telling It Like It Is* (Google Books, 2011).

7 Tom Peters, *In Search of Excellence* (Profile Books, 2015).

8 'As for working from home, "nine to five" is an anachronism in a creative and information-led economy. We will go back into offices but it won't be the same as before' – Max King, *MoneyWeek*, 15/5/2020.

9 We cited *Super Teams* in the Preface to this book and criticised it for its failure to address the motivation issue. But there is also wise advice to be found in its pages. This still seems timely: 'All the evidence suggests that, in order to improve teamworking across the organisation, you have to develop a critical mass of people in the organisation all thinking along the same lines to make any real difference. We would suggest five to ten per cent of the managerial population as a rule of thumb and a similar percentage of their salary bill invested in the process, if we are to make any real impact on improving Teamworking across the organisation as a whole' – Colin Hastings, Peter Bixby, Rani Chaudry-Lawton, of Ashridge Management College, *Super Teams: A Blueprint for Organisational Success* (Gower, 1986; Fontana Paperbacks, 2nd edition, 1988). This critical mass of people, we would add, needs to be focused on Mapping Motivation and using its language and metrics.

Resources

This section of the book is designed to help you find more information about motivation, engagement and Motivational Maps. It is not comprehensive and will be subsequently updated.

Information about Motivation Maps Ltd and Motivational Maps

Motivational Maps Ltd was founded in 2006. Its Motivational Map is ISO accredited: ISO 17065: www.irqao.com/PDF/C11364-51147.pdf

The company website can be found at www.motivationalmaps.com and enquiries should be addressed to info@motivationalmaps.com

There are currently four different Motivational Maps available:

1. The Motivational Map is for individuals and employees to discover what motivates them and how motivated they are; this produces a 15-page report on the individual.
2. The Motivational Team Map, which this book is largely devoted to. This is a 22+ page report which synthesises the individual maps from any number of people and reveals what the overall motivational scores are. It is ideal for team leaders and managers.
3. The Motivational Organisational Map produces a 44-page report and synthesises the information from any number of team maps be they from the whole organisation or a section of the whole organisation. Ideal for senior managers to understand how to implement their strategies through people.
4. The Motivational Youth Map is different from the other Maps in that it has three outputs: one for the student, one for the teacher and one for the parent; all designed to help motivate the student to succeed at school and college. Ideal for 11–18-year-olds and schools and colleges looking to motivate their students. There is also the Youth Group Map. It is also available in Hungarian.

The Motivational Map questionnaire is in nine different languages: English, Hungarian, Spanish, German, French, Italian, Greek, Lithuanian, and Portuguese.

Motivational Maps Ltd has licensed over 800 consultants, coaches and trainers to deliver the Map products in 15 countries. There are five Senior Practitioners of Maps in the UK.

UK Senior Practitioners

James Sale, the author, can be found at www.jamessale.co.uk
Dorset
His Linkedin profile is: https://uk.linkedin.com/in/jamesmotivationsale

Bevis Moynan, Magenta Coaching Solutions, www.magentac.co.uk
Cambridgeshire

Jane Thomas, Premier Life Skills, www.premierlifeskills.co.uk
Dorset

Carole Gaskell, Full Potential Group, https://www.fullpotentialgroup.co.uk
London

Kate Turner, Motivational Leadership, www.motivationalleadership.co.uk
Wiltshire

Susannah Brade-Waring and Heath Waring, Aspirin Business Solutions, www.aspirinbusiness.com
Dorset

Motivational Maps Resources can be found on www.motivationalmaps.com/Resources

For more information on Motivational Youth Maps contact:
Mark Turner at www.motivationalmapseducation.com and mark@motivationalmentoring.com

Other key books on motivation, team and organisational development

Twelve books we like on motivation, teams and organisational development:
  The Attitude Factor, Thomas Blakeslee (Thorsons, 1997)
  The Collected Papers of Roger Harrison (McGraw-Hill, 1995)
  Effective Change, Andrew Leigh (IPM, 1988)

Finding Meaning in the Second Half of Life, James Hollis (Penguin, 2006)

The Five Dysfunctions of a Team, Patrick Lencioni (Jossey-Bass, 2002)

The Handbook of Communication Training, edited J.D. Wallace (Routledge, 2019)

The Leadership Challenge, James Kouzes and Barry Posner (Jossey-Bass, 2002)

Life's Philosophy, Arne Naess (University of Georgia Press, 2002)

Management Teams, R. Meredith Belbin (Heinemann, 1985)

Managing Change and Making It Stick, Roger Plant (Fontana/Collins, 1987)

Organisational Development, edited Cliff Oswick and David Grant (Pitman, 1996)

The Spirit at Work Phenomenon, Sue Howard and David Welbourn (Azure, 2004)

TEAM REWARD STRATEGIES FOR THE DEFENDER – Relationship

1. Communicate – especially good news about the organisation and how it's doing. Use regular briefings, notice-board, even emails where necessary.
2. Link organisational goals and achievement to personal security. Do this informally and formally (for example, at appraisal time).
3. Reward and value loyalty and faithful service within the Defender team – be explicit about this. Stress team values and co-operation.
4. Define roles and responsibilities within the team clearly – remove ambiguity. The organisational chart is also a reassuring aide-memoir to have around.
5. Create and publish plans. Do things in incremental steps – safe and sure. Long term planning prevents fire-fighting and crisis management.
6. Provide perks that tap into their need for security – health care provisions, pension enhancements, loyalty schemes.
7. Create an environment where dependability is par for the course. For example, good furniture, hardware that is quality and functions.

TEAM REWARD STRATEGIES FOR THE FRIEND – Relationship

1. Organise good social events for the Friend team. Make sure it's one they want – ask! But also cultivate in spontaneity, appear 'natural'.
2. Make a good social working environment. Make sure access to people is easy and free. Avoid closed doors, no-go areas, forbidding plaques!
3. Publicly stick up for the Friend team when times get tough –they really appreciate it.

4. Consider the welfare of the Friend team. Is there a quiet room where they can go if they need to calm down, or rest, or meditate or nap?
5. Encourage peer-to-peer 'Now That' rewards ('Now That' you've achieved this, you get that). Enable anyone in the team to award.
6. Rotate low priority or low skill tasks around the team. This will lessen the boredom and increase the sense of sharing.
7. Regularly ask the team: What do you think [about X]? And where relevant and possible, take them into your confidence.

TEAM REWARD STRATEGIES FOR THE STAR – Relationship

1. Motivate the Star team with prestige and awards. The key thing about awards from the management perspective is to make them little and often.
2. Work on something as a team for charity. This work tends to be highly credible and usually high profile.
3. Produce a real organisational newsletter that is fun, fun, fun! Less boring stuff about your gizmo and more about Star team members.
4. Publicise – by advertising in newspapers and magazines – all industry awards that your organisation and Star team wins or is nominated for.
5. Create a display case – often called the 'Wow wall' – where letters and testimonials from satisfied customers are visible.
6. Invest in business cards for all staff, especially Star team members. This enhances their importance and provides marketing for your organisation.
7. Link ambitious targets for the Star team to high visibility rewards – Stars will go for it.

TEAM REWARD STRATEGIES FOR THE DIRECTOR – Achievement

1. Be explicit – ask the Director team who wants the leader's job? And build from there – empower them.
2. Delegate responsibilities to the Director team and monitor how they perform. Be sure you have safeguards; training is critical.
3. Give the team leadership coaching, mentoring and training. Directors need it in order to achieve the level of performance that they seek.
4. Allow Directors to stand in for the Team Leader as often as possible. This can be difficult, but this will really help team performance.
5. Create an atmosphere of performance and control – for example, does the furniture and office technology convey a sense of high performance?
6. Ask the Director team to review how successful meetings are within the organisation. Use this review to re-structure how meetings operate.
7. Invite team members to an organisational seminar entitled, 'Is management for me?' Enable them to think about their careers.

TEAM REWARD STRATEGIES FOR THE BUILDER – Achievement

1. Set clear goals and link them to rewards, especially financial ones. Team goal-setting is a powerful tool. Goals need to be clearly linked to rewards.
2. What one-off bonuses for extraordinary efforts and achievements are available? Find and use them – here they really count.
3. What other perks are possible and might motivate the Builder team? Consider small things. The motivators for £15 or less.
4. Engage the Builder team's competitive spirit. What games or competitions do you have organised on an ongoing basis?
5. Demonstrate to the Builder team that your organisation is financially astute. Builders like sound economic decisions since they appreciate the value of money.
6. Consider where you could offer Builder teams a discount on your products and services.
7. What extra training might help the Builder team become more valuable to the company and so entail a pay rise or a perk?

TEAM REWARD STRATEGIES FOR THE EXPERT – Achievement

1. Ensure an excellent induction programme for new Expert team members. A good start is likely to keep the Expert hooked.
2. Flag up learning opportunities over the next year for the team and individuals within it. Show them the overall development plan and what's on it for them.
3. Use Mentoring Opportunities. Experts will especially like mentoring from a more knowledgeable or skilled colleague and this can work within the team.
4. Invest in e-learning packages – technical, interpersonal and managerial – to enable staff to carry on learning 24/7.
5. Can the office environment be used as part of the learning environment? Consider display areas and the environment: how can they be utilised?
6. Give members of the team the opportunity to attend courses during the day, particularly if working for a degree level type of qualification.
7. Ask Experts within the team to share their learning experience – ask them to cascade their learning, especially after external courses.

TEAM REWARD STRATEGIES FOR THE CREATOR – Growth

1. Use creative techniques to generate ideas at team meetings – especially brainstorming, the 20 questions technique, or 6 Thinking Hats.
2. Identify all the business areas in which fresh input might be appropriate and beneficial. Get the team to work on them.

3. Set goals and objectives that specifically require creative applications or original solutions to challenging problems.
4. Avoid putting the Creators in a routine role or working on a routine project for too long a period. Routine invariably means 'boring' to the Creator.
5. Set aside a training day where all the team are expected to work on anything they choose (but which will benefit the organisation).
6. Offer the Creator team training and development that enables them to use and optimise their skills more creatively and more effectively.
7. Provide a stimulating environment – creative ideas are stimulated by beauty, by nature, by music and art, and often by what is unusual.

TEAM REWARD STRATEGIES FOR THE SPIRIT – Growth

1. Encourage the mind-set that the team is really a Managing Board of their own business. Bolster their self-image.
2. Increase the scope of the Spirit team's decision-making. Delegate to them, where appropriate. Reduce 'interference' in how they work.
3. Give them maximum control over how they utilise their time. They can work to a very tight schedule, but avoid arbitrarily imposed timetables.
4. Provide a relaxed environment – provide an office environment where the Spirit team feels relaxed and at home, rather than formally constrained.
5. Institute 'dress down' Fridays (or whatever day) in which the Spirit team can wear casual clothes (except perhaps when meeting customers or clients).
6. Let Spirit team members work at home! This is particularly the case where the technology and the role coincide.
7. Allocate 10% of time – one afternoon a week – to allow Spirit teams to work on their own projects and research which may benefit the organisation.

TEAM REWARD STRATEGIES FOR THE SEARCHER – Growth

1. Searcher teams love positive feedback – so give them it. Especially tell them about the consequences of their work and praise them.
2. Create a more stimulating environment around the Searcher. Think about: colour, rhythm, nature, light, art.
3. Avoid meaningless routines with Searcher teams. Review their current work flow. Ask for ideas on how to vary the work or the routines.

4. Obtain positive customer feedback for the Searcher team. They love testimonials and endorsements about the outcomes of their service.
5. Make sure that all equipment and materials the team uses are fit for purpose. Inadequate equipment and materials derail their purpose.
6. Improve regular communications at work: oral, written, electronic and use visual, oral and kinaesthetic modes to communicate.
7. Engage in team building exercises – develop a team culture. This re-enforces the significance of the Searcher team's work.

Index

Printed in the United States
By Bookmasters